Between the Lines

Between the Lines

A Philosophy of Theatre

MICHAEL Y. BENNETT

OXFORD
UNIVERSITY PRESS

Oxford University Press is a department of the University of Oxford.
It furthers the University's objective of excellence in research, scholarship,
and education by publishing worldwide. Oxford is a registered trademark of
Oxford University Press in the UK and in certain other countries.

Published in the United States of America by Oxford University Press
198 Madison Avenue, New York, NY 10016, United States of America.

© Oxford University Press 2024

All rights reserved. No part of this publication may be reproduced, stored in
a retrieval system, or transmitted, in any form or by any means, without the
prior permission in writing of Oxford University Press, or as expressly permitted
by law, by license, or under terms agreed with the appropriate reproduction
rights organization. Inquiries concerning reproduction outside the scope of the
above should be sent to the Rights Department, Oxford University Press, at the
address above.

You must not circulate this work in any other form and
you must impose this same condition on any acquirer.

Library of Congress Cataloging-in-Publication Data
Names: Bennett, Michael Y., 1980– author.
Title: Between the lines / Michael Y. Bennett.
Description: New York : Oxford University Press, 2024. |
Includes bibliographical references and index.
Identifiers: LCCN 2023057083 (print) | LCCN 2023057084 (ebook) |
ISBN 9780197691670 (hardback) | ISBN 9780197691694 |
ISBN 9780197691700 | ISBN 9780197691687 (epub)
Subjects: LCSH: Theater—Philosophy.
Classification: LCC PN2039 .B45535 2024 (print) | LCC PN2039 (ebook) |
DDC 792.01—dc23/eng/20240116
LC record available at https://lccn.loc.gov/2023057083
LC ebook record available at https://lccn.loc.gov/2023057084

DOI: 10.1093/9780197691700.001.0001

Printed by Integrated Books International, United States of America

For my sons, Maxwell and Julius—
It always was, is, and will be, for you . . .

Contents

Acknowledgments	ix
Introduction: The Conceptual Spaces of Theatre	1

PART I PIECES OF THEATRE: DEFINING THEATRE AND ITS EMPTY SPACES

1. Previous Conceptions of Theatre	15
2. The Nature of Theatre	33
3. The Nature of Viewing Theatre	55
4. The Nature of Theatre's Empty Spaces	73

PART II SPACES OF THEATRE: OFFSTAGE CHARACTERS, IMAGINED OBJECTS, AND OTHER PRICKLY PHILOSOPHICAL PROBLEMS IN THEATRE

5. Distinctness in Theatre: Theatrical Language and Events	87
6. Subsumption in Theatre: The Question of Lady Bracknell's Nose and Offstage Characters	109
7. Truthfulness in Theatre: Imagined Objects and Actors and Acting	125

viii   CONTENTS

Conclusion: *Theatri Topia* for the Curious   141

Glossary   151
Notes   155
Bibliography   173
Index   185

Acknowledgments

This book has been the culmination of over a decade of my work on theatre studies and philosophy. As such, I have numerous people to thank (as in a sense, every person who helped me with all my scholarship over the past decade-plus), but most especially the following scholars (in alphabetical order) for their incisive feedback at many different stages of this specific book: Susan Feagin (Temple University); David Friedell (Union College); James R. Hamilton (Kansas State University); John Mackay (University of Wisconsin-Madison); Alan Sidelle (University of Wisconsin-Madison); and Karen Simecek (University of Warwick). I also want to thank Clare Hall (University of Cambridge) for providing an amazing intellectual environment in which I was able to draft much of this book, as well as thank my fellow Visiting Fellows and now friends: Juan Pablo Heras, Diana Carrió-Invernizzi, Hayden Bellenoit, Sara Vakhshouri, Cameron Buckner, Lindita Camaj, Anuj Bhuwania, Malini Aisola, Leslie Carlin, and Simon M. Coleman. Finally, I want to thank my wonderful editor at Oxford University Press, Lucy Randall, for her constant enthusiasm for this book, from submission all the way through to publication.

As for the book itself, I would like to thank the following publishers and journals for letting me use some previously published material: *Philosophy and Literature* for allowing me to reprint two articles, "In Defense of Abstract Creationism: A Recombinatorial Approach," which comprises a part of Chapter 2, and "Intrinsic-Extrinsic Properties in Theatre," which comprises a part of Chapter 7; *Journal of Literary Semantics* for allowing me to reprint my article, "Propositions in Theatre: Theatrical Utterances

x ACKNOWLEDGMENTS

as Events," which comprises part of Chapter 5; *Oxford Bibliographies* for allowing me to reprint some small sections from my article, "Philosophy of Theater," found in Chapter 1; Routledge for allowing me to reprint some small sections of my book, *Analytic Philosophy and the World of the Play* (2017) in Chapters 2 and 5 and some small sections of *The Problems of Viewing Performance: Epistemology and Other Minds* (2021) in Chapter 3; and Palgrave Macmillan for allowing me to reprint a very small section of *Narrating the Past through Theatre: Four Crucial Texts* (2012) in the Conclusion.

Of course, a book like this cannot be completed, or even take off, without the help of friends, family, and loved ones. I want to start by thanking my parents, Jeffrey and Debra Bennett, as well as my sister, Anna Bennett, and my brother-in-law, Steven M. Fischer, for their steadfast love and support, as well as my closest friends over the past decade or more: Eyal Tamir, Colin Enriquez, Joel Anderson, Jeremy Church, Shai Cohen, Lauren Roth, Mike Musgrave, Steve Rosenlund, Stephen Lommele, Katie Bond, Louis Betty, Maija Birenbaum, Tanya Kam, and Elena Levy-Navarro. Now, too, I get to add my love, Carrie, and her son, Cole, to this list of amazing people who have made this book what it is. Ultimately, though, my sons, Maxwell and Julius, have been my guiding light over the past decade of my life: you are both my everything, and I love you more than you can ever imagine.

Introduction
The Conceptual Spaces of Theatre

A Spell

An elongated and heightened (*Rest*). Denoted by repetition of figures' names with no dialogue. Has sort of an architectural look:

Lincoln
Booth
Lincoln
Booth

This is a place where the figures experience their pure true simple state. While no action or stage business is necessary, directors should fill this moment as they best see fit.[1]

In her 2002 Pulitzer Prize–winning play, *Topdog/Underdog*, Suzan-Lori Parks describes, in this epigraph, what she calls "a spell," which is to be used as an "unconventional theatrical element" (3). Lincoln and Booth, the play's only two characters, are African American brothers and roommates named as such by their father, which "was his idea of a joke" (Parks 2001: 24). Centered on the *hustle*—three-card monte (which I will revisit in the Conclusion)—Lincoln and Booth are trying to make ends meet in a racist and unforgiving world. Lincoln starts the play trying to survive through hard work in an honest, though ironic, job: dressing up as Abraham Lincoln to let people pretend to shoot him. Booth, however, is stealing to get

Between the Lines. Michael Y. Bennett, Oxford University Press. © Oxford University Press 2024.
DOI: 10.1093/9780197691700.003.0001

2 BETWEEN THE LINES

by. In the end, neither can escape the pull and the danger of three-card monte, with its promise of easy money, which leads to Booth prophetically killing Lincoln.

In part stage direction, in part speech heading with no speeches/dialogue, these "spell[s]" provide the director and likely the actors with a creative vacuum to be filled in for performance, but also for the reader and their imagination. But these spells are unlike common stage directions, with stage directions the subject of the (recent and excellent) similarly titled book, *The Lines Between the Lines*, by Bess Rowen (2021). Normally, stage directions provide information not available to the readers or to the actors and directors that are needed to put on a performance (or imagine the play when reading it). To be utterly clear, this is not a book about stage directions. Instead, Parks's "spell[s]," though, can only make sense based upon what we know from the rest of the play, itself, and as a conceptual empty space, the characters/"figures" in their "spell[s]" get to the heart of how theatre operates, begging two questions for this book: *What is the relationship between theatre's words and the (conceptual) empty spaces between the lines?* and *How does this relationship play out with real bodies, in real space, moving through real time, both in performance and in the readers' imaginations?*

Building upon my previous work on the ontology of theatre (esp. Bennett 2017) and the epistemology of theatre (esp. Bennett 2012, 2021), here I examine theatre through its (conceptual) empty spaces. As such, I will be culling previous ideas and combining them with many more new ones, the latter, especially, coming from the field of philosophical semantics, particularly the idea of subsumption. In thinking about the conceptual empty spaces of theatre, I will be investigating three main topics within this book: (1) *theatre as an art form*, (2) *the properties of theatrical characters and theatrical worlds*, and (3) *the difference between truth and truthfulness in the theatre*. Ultimately, this book aims to offer the first (contemporary) *systematic account of theatre*—thinking about theatre metaphysically, epistemologically, and ethically (the last, only in terms of value).

INTRODUCTION 3

While this book is not attempting to describe *why* an object is considered art, to better understand theatre, it may be helpful to begin by asking, what types of objects are (considered to be) art?[2] Let us begin with a working list that excludes theatre, for just a second:

Word-based art (e.g., literature, poetry, film, television, etc.)
Sound-based art (e.g., lyrical music, instrumental music, electronic music, etc.)
Body-based art (e.g., dance, some performance art, etc.)
Image-based art (e.g., painting, sculpture, photography, etc.)
Object-based art (e.g., architecture, design, etc.)

First, let me be the first to acknowledge that there is, of course, plenty of overlap among these categories. But categorizing and labeling are important in regard to art, in some part, precisely so artists can push against the previously established norms and against the very categories and labels that were created or changed on account of a (somewhat imaginary) catalog of previous pieces of art.

One key and important feature of theatre, to turn to our subject at hand, is that theatre often incorporates all of the main features of other art forms:

Word-based art (e.g., speeches in theatre)
Sound-based art (e.g., sound and/or musical score in theatre)
Body-based art (e.g., actors in theatre)
Image-based art (e.g., scenic design in theatre)
Object-based art (e.g., props in theatre)

But this is not what, necessarily, makes theatre unique. What makes theatre unique among various art forms is that so much of the art form is not *in* the art, itself, but is a product or, maybe, a by-product of the art. That is not to say that the text is the art and the performance of a text is the practice of the art, per se, but that

4 BETWEEN THE LINES

within both of these, the fleshing out of the art happens by what is not specified in the art itself. That is, *much of theatre resides between the lines.*

Above, I used "between the lines" in a figurative manner. However, to be more explicit in my claims, the only tangible remnants from the dramatic text in performance are the spoken words/speeches of each character. And while there are stage directions in the play, if even followed, the viewers of a play may or may not know they exist in the play. However, and to somewhat contrast with W. B. Worthen's view that the words of a play are a "tool" or instrument for performance,[3] most of the viewing experience is not simply an auditory one that centers on the spoken words that populate the majority of the written play. Real bodies, in real space, doing real actions make up the majority of theatrical performance. And this is true, too, to a degree in the reading process of drama, where the reader imagines real bodies, in real space, doing real action based upon just words (and in the reading process you get the benefit of some stage directions). That is, the words of the play are only a part of the production and the reading of the play, and this is rather unique among various art forms, as the play originates from the dramatic text, which is also an integral part of theatre, and it can be enjoyed on its own. This is one place where theatre departs from film, as screenplays are not read by the average filmgoer, whereas it is much more likely that a theatregoer may have read the play.

To investigate theatre and its in-between spaces, this book will introduce some basic ideas about *coherence* and *correspondence* and, much more prominently, conversations surrounding *subsumption* and *distinctness* to better describe the art form. Instead of limiting the concept and use of subsumption to suggest that *constituent parts* are subsumed within a distinct whole (as is done in philosophical semantics, from where subsumption comes from), here in this book, I broaden the concept to claim that many of the *properties* of a theatrical character and/or a theatrical world are subsumed within the text. Unlike how fiction has a narrator that generally describes the properties of literary characters, theatre (particularly for the theatregoer) is largely devoid of distinct properties attributed to theatrical characters. Outside of the fact that character x says "_____" and does _____, with its corresponding properties being, character x has the properties of *being the speaker of* "_____" and *being the doer of* _____, there are few, if any, specified properties regarding theatrical characters and/or theatrical worlds. But, of course, it is difficult (though not impossible) to argue that theatrical characters (and/or theatrical worlds) do not have properties associated with them. Thinking about how the study of properties is also one of relations, along these same lines, I will examine, too, how objects are re-positioned with/against one another to create (or "re-create") fictional objects in the theatre to offer a novel way to make sense of what is and what is not specified in theatre.

Organization of the Book

In short, Part I (i.e., Chapters 1–4) lays out the claims of the book; Part II (i.e., Chapters 5–7) provides specific cases where the conceptual empty spaces in theatre beg further investigation. Part I moves from (1) noting how theatre has previously been conceived, to (2) describing the nature of theatre, to (3) describing the nature of viewing theatre, and finally to (4) describing the empty spaces of theatre (both ontologically and epistemologically). In Part II, Chapter 5 deals with *distinct* facts and the spaces in between those facts: speeches in theatre and historical facts in history plays. Chapter 6 looks at what is *subsumed* by the theatrical text: which properties are intrinsic and/or extrinsic to theatrical characters and offstage characters. And Chapter 7 examines not necessarily what is true in theatre but what is *truthful*: imagined objects and truthfulness in acting. While the issues explored in each chapter in Part

6 BETWEEN THE LINES

II originate with distinctness, subsumption, and truthfulness, respectively, there are many overlapping discussions across all three chapters. This book closes with a Conclusion about constants and variables in games, the rules of engagement in theatre, and finally how theatre promotes curious behaviors.

Again, over the course of the four chapters that comprise "Part I: Pieces of Theatre: Defining Theatre and Its Empty Spaces," I lay out the overarching claims of the book. In Chapter 1, I turn to the nature of theatre and how previous scholars, thinkers, and philosophers have categorized and understood this art form. I trace the history of definitions (and categorizations) from Plato and Aristotle to the present day.

Chapter 2 is concerned with the ontology of theatre. This chapter re-examines my previously developed claims that theatrical characters (all the way up to theatrical worlds) are a type of abstract object that I call a "re-creation." Re-creation explains the ontological status of theatre and is similar to D. M. Armstrong's recombinatorial possibilia. But to these previous claims, I also want to add another dimension, one that takes into account a larger range of performances: "re-positioned objects." That is, re-creation does not do as adequate a job alone in explaining performances that are less story-book-like. Many theatrical performances (broadly conceived) only examine existent objects, but they do so from previously unexplored vantage points. In this chapter, I examine this relational-recombinatorial view of theatre by thinking about metaphor, representation, and presentation. In the first section of this chapter, "Metaphor in Theatre," I examine one of the most fundamental devices in the arts: metaphor. Along with simile and allegory, metaphor forms the backbone of fiction, broadly conceived. This chapter will examine how metaphor has been conceived. Further, this chapter will also look at how we can better conceive metaphor to describe more accurately what is happening in theatre through re-creation. This chapter will raise the point that if a metaphor referred, or were likened, to a referent(s) outside of the text, then it becomes an allegory and/or an analogy. However, literature—broadly defined to include fiction, drama (and theatre), and poetry—works precisely because there is *no specific* referent or likening. It is also precisely because of the *loose* connection between a word and its cluster of associations that *fiction* (versus a description of reality) can occur. In the second part, "Representation in Theatre," I look at how theatre employs representation. While *metaphor* largely makes use of re-creation, much of *representation* in the theatre makes use of the re-positioning of objects to help us better understand and explore something true and/or truthful. This chapter looks back at the literature surrounding theatre as a representational art form to demonstrate how representation works in the theatre. That is, this chapter will suggest that the concept described earlier of re-positioned objects/ideas creates the intellectual thrust of representation in the theatre and how it operates. And in the final section, "Presentation in Theatre," I look at *presentation* in the theatre, and cases of it, where elements of re-creation and re-positioning sit side by side. Presentation, it will be claimed, adopts the techniques and tools from both metaphor and representation to *show* (something). Presentation is where much of performance art falls, as well as, often, one-person shows.

Chapter 3 is concerned with the epistemology of theatre. Much of this is culled from my last book, *The Problems of Viewing Performance: Epistemology and Other Minds* (2021). Here, I streamline the concept, for this book's present purposes, of individual and group triangulation that is needed to understand a performance, as witnessed by two or more viewers. I turn to ideas about Bayesian epistemology to explain how different viewers of a performance do not share the same experiences. That is, while performance may be a public event, performance is not a shared individual experience, as viewers not only come in with differing amounts and types of knowledge but also will be looking for different amounts and types of information during the performance. Given that I claim a piece

8   BETWEEN THE LINES

of theatre never really ends, I discuss how theatre is a living document and a malleable idea.

Chapter 4 adds the idea to examine theatre through its empty spaces by thinking through theatre through the here-revised concepts of subsumption and distinctness as used in philosophical semantics. What makes theatre so unique among various art forms is that so much of the art form is not *in* the art itself but is a product or by-product of the art. That is not to say that the text is the art and the performance of a text is the practice of the art, per se, but that within both of these, the fleshing out of the art happens by what is not specified in the art itself. That is, *much of theatre resides between the lines.* The main idea here is that all of the *properties* of all characters and the theatrical worlds have to be located somewhere, even though most of those properties are not distinctly stated in the spoken words of a theatrical performance. To investigate theatre and its in-between spaces, this book will introduce conversations in philosophical semantics surrounding *subsumption* and *distinctness.* Broadening the concept and use of subsumption past the way it is understood and used in philosophical semantics, where it is claimed that *constituent parts* are subsumed within a distinct whole, I claim that many of the *properties* of a theatrical character and/or a theatrical world are subsumed within the text. I claim that there are three *types of properties* associated with theatrical characters and worlds: *distinct properties, subsumed properties,* and *truthful properties.* That is, theatrical characters have properties that go beyond what is in the text, and that these properties are derived— via entailment, actual generic connections, and/or whole/parts connections—from the text in combination with facts about the actual world.

The second part of the book, "Part II: Spaces of Theatre: Offstage Characters, Imagined Objects, and Other Prickly Philosophical Problems," looks at specific and special situations or cases that relate to the blank spaces of theatre surrounding questions of, primarily, ontology and epistemology: in essence, Part II applies

INTRODUCTION 9

the claims from Chapters 2–4 to examine a number of prickly problems in the theatre that are related to issues surrounding distinctness, subsumption, and truthfulness. Chapter 5, "Distinctness in the Theatre: Theatrical Language as Events," I look at the language uttered in the play, as, in addition to what the characters *do*, what the characters *say* constitutes one of the few distinct facts found in a play. This chapter examines particular language usage in theatre using William Shakespeare's *Hamlet* and the play within the play, *The Murder of Gonzago*, as a case study. This essay argues that theatrical utterances constitute a special case of language usage not previously elucidated: the utterance of a statement with propositional content in theatre functions as an event. In short, the propositional content of a particular p (e.g., p_1, p_2, p_3 . . .), whether or not it is true, is only understood—and understood to be true—if p_1 is uttered in a particular time, place, and situation (i.e., during a theatrical event); otherwise, the propositional content in those theatrical utterances can either be false or contingently true. A history play, or a play that invokes historical events, is generally based upon a set of distinct facts, often about an object (often a person) and/or an event. Outside of those usually quite limited number of distinct facts (dates, names, such and such events, etc.), most of the truthfulness of a play comes from a set of subsumed properties that are not (necessarily) *true*, but display, rather, truthfulness.

Thinking about what is true and contained in the play and what is not true and not contained in the play, Chapter 6, "Subsumption in the Theatre: The Question of Lady Bracknell's Nose and Offstage Characters," claims that theatre problematizes intrinsic and extrinsic properties in the theatre. David Friedell has recently discussed the relationship between intrinsic and extrinsic properties of art, specifically in music. Friedell claims that normative social rules dictate who can change the intrinsic or extrinsic properties of a piece of music. I claim that in text-based theatre—as a particular art form—the dividing line between intrinsic and extrinsic properties of a play is sometimes tenuous. This tenuousness

10 BETWEEN THE LINES

is due to a play's bifurcated existence as a dramatic text and as many theatrical performances. Moving from investigating the truth found in a play to thinking about a problematic character type, I examine a problem case that the offstage character poses for conversations surrounding indeterminate identity. In claiming that abstract creationism can be committed to indeterminate identity, David Friedell (2019) has recently argued against R. Woodward's (2017) claim that while there is such a thing as indeterminate reference, there is no indeterminate identity. Friedell (2019) suggests that whether fictional realism entails that there is indeterminate identity depends upon what fictional characters are. In this chapter, I claim that there is indeterminate identity in fictional characters, suggesting that the case of theatre is important to consider when discussing both indeterminate identity and the ontology of fictional characters. I will do this, then, by considering another case of a fictional character: the offstage character in theatre. I would like to join this conversation—which, thus far, has mostly focused on largely generic fictional entities—by claiming that examining theatre's most famous offstage character, Godot, in Samuel Beckett's *Waiting for Godot* (1954), presents a somewhat different problem case about indeterminate identity. In this chapter, I examine indeterminate identity, not by asking whether two characters can be identical, but by claiming that it is indeterminate whether the offstage character, Godot, can correspond to multiple fictional entities.

While the character of Godot exists as something of an abstract object, there are things that do not exist in the play that are of vital importance to the experience of a play. In Chapter 7, "Truthfulness in the Theatre: Actor and Acting and Imagined Objects," I examine how theatre relies and deals with imagination. Beginning by asking, "Who is Hamlet?" which is a question that has, for centuries, been asked and never fully (or satisfactorily) been definitively answered, what if, rather, we ask, "Who *cannot* be Hamlet?" By thinking about acting and the character through the concepts of *subsumption* and *distinctness* (as used in philosophical semantics), this chapter is

INTRODUCTION   11

not trying to define a theatrical character by way of the negative. What asking this question does do, rather, is create a spectrum where "Who *is* Hamlet?" and "Who *cannot be* Hamlet?" are the two poles that contain distinct properties (that either distinctly define who Hamlet is or are properties that are distinctly *not*-Hamlet). But these two poles are less of the concern of this essay, as between these poles (i.e., on this spectrum), however, I claim, are all the *subsumed properties* within the character of Hamlet. Investigating the subsumed properties of a character helps thread the needle between something that is necessarily *true* versus something that is *truthful*. In *The Art of Theater* (2007), James R. Hamilton suggests that by understanding precedence and projecting salient features of the performance—and by understanding that everyone else is doing the same thing—that spectators all come to possess a rough common knowledge of the same events. While Hamilton (and the work, too, of Jerrold Levinson, Tzachi Zamir, and Noël Carroll) aids in the understanding of a *concrete* object, what about the uninvestigated spaces of theatrical stages that have not been experienced and/or do not exist, except in the imagination of, say, audience members? It is not just, for example, offstage characters that are caught in the crosshairs of the imagination of the different viewers; so, too, whether passively or actively, the empty spaces of the stage are often filled in more completely by imagination. Importantly, multiple viewers are all doing this, too.

I conclude by thinking ethically—about value in, and the value of, theatre—in "*Teatri Topia* for the Curious: Constants, Variables, Play, and Theatre's Rules of Engagement," by suggesting that because of the many empty conceptual spaces in theatre that both participating in and watching theatre require and encourage curious behaviors. In investigating what curiosity is and how theatre helps develop individually and societally needed curious behaviors, I liken theatre to some games that are found in some well-known plays (e.g., card games, chess, etc.). Despite objections raised, and that curiosity has mostly been seen as a mental process

12 BETWEEN THE LINES

or drive by philosophers, psychologists, and neuroscientists, I claim that curiosity refers to a *cluster of different behaviors* that are all loosely connected to the creation and/or acquisition of knowledge. By thinking about how the blank spaces of theatre require both participants and viewers to create and/or acquire knowledge, I conclude by considering how theatre, itself, promotes curious behaviors.

PART I
PIECES OF THEATRE
Defining Theatre and Its Empty Spaces

PART 1

1
Previous Conceptions of Theatre

Before beginning to develop the claims of this book, I want to provide a review of how theatre has previously been conceived. However, even before I venture forth to amass a collection of thoughts by others, I would say that I should establish what I mean, generally, by "theatre," as how I define it here helps us understand the purview of the present book. I will invoke and examine two general types of theatre which I am including under the umbrella of "theatre": (1) plays that have a dramatic text and whose theatrical performance are based on[1] the dramatic text (e.g., traditional text-based theatre) and (2) performances based on some form of script (broadly defined) that are billed as, or implied to be, theatre that are staged in a theatre venue or designated theatre space (e.g., site-specific performances, one-person shows, devised theatre, docudrama, verbatim theatre, etc.). Both of these types give a lot of wiggle room in which plays and performances fall under this two-pronged umbrella, as these two are certainly not hermetically sealed, nor even quite accepted, categories. However, the very nature of art, broadly defined, is in a constant state of change, as iconoclasts of each art form both expand the categories and also delimit and/or delineate these categories through creating a sufficient-enough departure from the previously understood categories (Bennett 2017: 19–21).

Theatre—that is, traditional text-based theatre—is widely considered the art form that most closely resembles lived life: real bodies in real space play out a story through the actual passage of time. Because of this, theatre has long been a laboratory of, and for,

---

Between the Lines. Michael Y. Bennett, Oxford University Press. © Oxford University Press 2024.
DOI: 10.1093/9780197691700.003.0002

16 BETWEEN THE LINES

philosophical thought and reflection. The study of philosophy and theatre has a history that dates to, and flourished in, ancient Greece and Rome. While philosophers over the centuries have revisited the study of theatre, in particular, the past four decades have seen a noted and substantial increase of scholarship investigating the intersection of philosophy and theatre.

"Philosophy of theatre" is, on one hand, an amorphous concept; on the other hand, it is an ever-growing, recognized subfield both of analytic aesthetics and of theatre and performance studies. Philosophy of theatre is also sometimes referred to—or subsumed, more broadly, within—an emerging field called "performance philosophy." Whatever we aim to call the field, scholarship has coalesced around some fundamental preoccupations, which are not too dissimilar to questions that arise in other philosophies of [*fill-in-the-blank*] (e.g., art, music, film, dance, etc.). The debates in philosophy of theatre mostly fall into three branches of philosophy: ontology, epistemology, and aesthetics.

The major ontological debates center on liveness and the ephemeral nature of theatre, as well as the question, What is theatre? Epistemological studies examine audience reception and how meaning is made and/or transmitted. Finally, studies in aesthetics focus on two main questions: What is the relationship between dramatic text and theatrical performance? and What is the value of theatre? Like many in academia who are either in philosophy or feel its touch, philosophy of theatre is not without its principal divisions along the analytic-Continental lines. More particular to philosophy of theatre, a second division finds those aligned by who focus primarily on either the dramatic text (often, in literature departments) or the practice/production of theatrical performance (often, in theatre and/or performance departments).

The Approach to Theatre by Different Philosophical Branches

Ontology of Theatre

The basic question, What is theatre? still remains one of the most debated subjects in philosophy of theatre. Plato and Aristotle had ideas about mimesis and imitation, and this was taken up again in the 1960s (by Auerbach, most notably). There is also significant, though not fully direct commentary about this, much from the field of aesthetics, on questions of representation in the arts (e.g., Goodman 1968, 1978; Walton 1990; Wollheim 1980). Questions about the ontology of theatre have been raised via modal logic, particularly the "possible worlds" thesis (Degani-Raz 2003, 2005; Bennett 2017), which looked back to studies on fictional entities (too numerous to mention here, but the major texts are, as relating to philosophy of theatre, Kripke 1980, 2011; Pavel 1985; and Thomasson 1999). As theatre happens in front of an audience, What is an audience? is another question that is ontologically oriented toward the theatre. Studies have examined the necessity of audience, the relationship between audience and actors, and the composition of audience (e.g., Blau 1990; S. Bennett 1990; Bennett 2012). Finally, given that theatre happens in the "here and now," one of the central issues to philosophy of theatre concerns "liveness" and ephemerality: from debates as to whether or how to document theatre (Phalen 1993; Auslander 1999) to the idea of "ghosting" (Carlson 2003) to trying to describe the nature of the ephemeral (States 1983, 1985; Zarrilli 2004; Fischer-Lichte 1992, 2008).

Epistemology of Theatre

Meaning and interpretation have been central to the industry of professional theatre scholarship. Much of this started with

18 BETWEEN THE LINES

Truth and Method (Gadamer 1960), but in philosophy of theatre, semiotics took hold in the 1970s to 1990s, as mentioned above. Two related questions occupied, and still occupy, philosophy of theatre: reception studies and reading texts versus "reading" performance (e.g., Carlson 1990; Elam 1980; S. Bennett 1990). Of all subfields in philosophy of theatre, the phenomenology of theatre is arguably the most written about. Much is due to both Bert O. States's 1985 book, *Great Reckonings in Little Rooms: On the Phenomenology of Theatre*, and, further, "Continental" philosophy's exploding influence on literature departments around that same time.

Aesthetics of Theatre

The relationship between text and performance has been at the forefront in debates around the aesthetics of theatre. Questions remain about whether dramatic literature and theatrical performance are independent or dependent art forms (Carroll 2001; Hamilton 2001; Saltz 2001). Also, there are ideas about how to describe the relationship: token-type (Dilworth 2002), score (Goodman 1968), or other ways (Worthen 2010). Finally, the value of theatre has long been a cultural war that seesaws throughout Western history: ancient Greece and Rome, Medieval (distrust), Renaissance, Puritans (distrust), Enlightenment, and so on. Recently, however, in large part because of the "decline of the humanities" (whether real or perceived), there is renewed interest in value (for the first contemporary sustained book-length study on the value of theatre, see Woodruff 2008). Value and ethics also find their way into recent discussions about the societal value of theatre (Dolan 2005).

The Approach to Theatre by Era

Classical Antiquity

Ancient Greece was pivotal in the arts and humanities, not only for its philosophy and theatre, separately, but for its philosophical introspection on its own art forms (most particularly, theatre). For well over two thousand years, Aristotle's *Poetics* has continued to inform and dominate the field of theatre studies and philosophy of theatre. Furthermore, not only are Plato's ideas on the theatre important, but Plato's dialogic form of writing has received new interest in twenty-first-century philosophy of theatre (see, particularly, Puchner 2010; Rokem 2010). The study of philosophy of theatre in ancient Rome was taken up, most notably and most influentially, by Seneca and Horace, who both looked to Aristotle's *Poetics* as central to their respective interests in form and rhetoric (for a history of the legacy of, particularly Aristotle and Horace, see Carlson 1993). A key text that is more practical than the more theoretical *Poetics* of Aristotle, Horace's text suggests that the dramatist must *instruct and delight* the audience (sometimes, though, translated as "instruct *or* delight"). Horace is interested in verisimilitude and differentiating dialogue that appropriately mirrors the position and disposition of the character.

Modern

As stated above, the entire field of the philosophy of theatre begins with Plato, and even more so, Aristotle, and moves through Horace's *Ars Poetica* (c. 15 BCE). These Greek and Roman pillars of thought on the theatre occupied, and continue to occupy, scholars over the millennia, but they certainly were central to thinkers through the Renaissance. From the beginning of the Enlightenment

20 BETWEEN THE LINES

through the nineteenth century, various other philosophers made significant contributions: Coleridge, Diderot, Hegel, Nietzsche, Rousseau, and Schiller.

Recently, the importance that French Enlightenment thinkers had on theatre has received much attention, from Descartes (Gobert 2013) to Voltaire and Diderot (Camp 2014). Nineteenth-century (especially, German) philosophers/writers—Nietzsche, Hegel, Goethe, and Schiller, among others—were integral to developing Romantic notions of theatre, which heavily informed and influenced the emergence of theatrical realism. Nietzsche's *The Birth of Tragedy* is, arguably, after Aristotle's *Poetics*, the most important and influential book on theatre. Recent books have re-examined Nietzsche's legacy in modern theatre (Kornhaber 2016; see also Bixby 2022).

Contemporary

There have been three recent, somewhat distinct "movements": (1) the study of semiotics and theatre in the 1970s–1990s; (2) the rise of performance studies in the 1990s, drawing much inspiration from Continental philosophers; and (3) the "philosophical turn" in theatre studies that took hold in the new millennium. Semiotics, which dominated studies in theatre theory from the 1970s to 1990s, rose concurrently with the growth of theories on structuralism and poststructuralism in literary studies (e.g., Carlson 1990; Elam 1980; S. Bennett 1990). Performance studies, developed in the 1990s and still a dominant field of theatre studies—or, in some ways, is now such an integral part of theatre studies that often the field is both called and thought of as "theatre and performance studies." Performance studies emerged with the concurrent rise cultural studies and "critical theory"/Continental philosophy in literature departments and the rise in performance art. Much is also related to feminist and queer philosophers (e.g., Dolan, Case, and Phelan).

The 2000s have seen what many have called the "philosophical turn" in theatre studies. The emergence and explosion of studies in philosophy and theatre in the new millennium have an important start in the *Journal of Aesthetics and Art Criticism*, in a 2001 special section debating the relationship between text and performance (Carroll 2001; Hamilton 2001; Saltz 2001). The 2006 collection, *Staging Philosophy*, is the first book to specifically investigate the overlap between philosophy and theatre (Krasner and Saltz 2006). A number of monographs followed over the next decade examining the overlap between philosophy and theatre (e.g., Hamilton 2007; Woodruff 2008; Rokem 2010; Puchner 2010; Bennett 2012, 2017; Gobert 2013; Golub 2014; Camp 2014; Stern 2014, 2017). Finally, the 2010s have seen the emergence of "performance philosophy," which is in part an offshoot of, in part subsumes, and in part just another name to call philosophy of theatre, though "performance philosophy" is decidedly organic and, thus, not quite a formal designation. "Performance philosophy" is the name of a discipline and the name of (all the same name) an online research network with over 2,500 members (https://performancephilosophy.org), a peer-reviewed online journal, and a book series.

Models of Theatre

Mimesis

As is the case with many philosophical discussions, the history of scholarly conversations begins (and continues on) with Plato and Aristotle. Plato's animus toward theatre and acting, mostly found in his *Republic*, Book X (c. 370 BCE), focuses on mimesis by way of ideas about *imitation* and his distrust of the theatre arts with the negative effects theatre has on society, followed by such tracts as Francis Bacon's "Idols of the Theatre" (1620) and Jean-Jacques Rousseau's "Discourse" (1750). Aristotle's *Poetics* (c. 330 BCE),

22 BETWEEN THE LINES

however, focuses largely on *mimesis* and still remains one of the foundational texts of theatre theorists, having been so, largely, throughout the centuries. While the question over the value of the theatre is no longer a question (e.g., see Paul Woodruff's *The Necessity of Theater* [2008]), the debates over ideas about imitation, pretense, and mimesis form a vital spine to this day surrounding philosophical ideas about acting and theatre as a whole.

The strength of this model—that is, mimesis—is that it is a familiar conceit, and while many types of theatre exist to the contrary, mimetic theatre *does* look and feel like real life, mirroring the embodied *liveness* of lived life.[2] That is, in theatrical performance, real bodies move through actual space and progress through actual time. However, of course, the exceptions to mimetic theatre are some of the very reasons that this mimetic model of theatre falls apart, as so much of contemporary theatre and performance does not attempt to be mimetic. In fact, many of the major theatre theorists of the twentieth century, such as E. Gordon Craig and Bertolt Brecht (to name simply the most obvious), have actively sought ways in which to expose the theatre to its own artifice.

Further, what is on the page and on the stage is not a mirror of nature (is not a reflection of the actual) but a (fictitious) re-creation of the actual, embodying concrete objects and actions, but in a way that the combination of these concrete objects and actions does not actually exist (and, hence, the *fictional* nature of fiction and theatre). That is, as I suggest in Bennett (2017), there is no way to reflect a fictional object back in a mirror. Mirrors and mimesis can only reflect what actually exists, and thus the mirror and mimetic model fall apart when faced with fiction (or, again, "re-creation").

Scores, Blueprints, Scripts

In his seminal book on the philosophy of art, *Languages of Art* (1968), Nelson Goodman develops how to think about "two-stage art forms," which include theatre. Goodman works through the ideas of the text (i.e., the first stage) as the score, blueprint, or script for the performance (i.e., the second stage). While somewhat attractive for its simplicity, these models create a clear hierarchy of the primacy of the text to the (afterthought of) performance. Related to this, though not exactly the same, we can add the newer idea of an "*ingredients* model," where theatre artists take the so-conceived "ingredients" from a dramatic text and *cook* them into final product (i.e., the performance).[3] To be clear, the "ingredients" model is an epistemic one, particularly Hamilton's version of it, and its use is to claim that theatrical performance is an independent art form, not merely a once-removed, or "second-stage," art form in relationship to the dramatic text.

These ideas about scores, blueprints, and scripts that created this idea about a "two-stage art form" were behind the now-seminal debates in the then-inchoate field of philosophy of theatre, where philosophers and theatre theorists debated the relationship between the dramatic text and theatrical performance, some thinking that the text was primary and others that the performance was its own art form (Carroll 2001; Saltz 2001; Hamilton 2001, 2007).[4] In my book *Analytic Philosophy and the World of the Play* (2017), I largely develop the blueprint model but attempt to do so without creating a hierarchy of the relationship between the text and the performance, as the dramatic text and theatrical performances are all "re-creations."

Types and Tokens

The idea of *types* and *tokens*, a stalwart concept found in many subfields in philosophy, was introduced to philosophical discussions surrounding the theatre largely by John Dilworth around the turn of the twenty-first century. The type-token model was one that also feeds into the above-mentioned debate about the

24 BETWEEN THE LINES

relationship between dramatic text and theatrical performance, as Dilworth (2002, 2002) suggests that the text is the type and the various performances are tokens of the type. In short, and without being too simplistic, the type is an idea/ideal (or *universal*), whereas tokens are individual instances (or *particulars*) of the type.

While attractive, as well, for its simplicity and ease of describing the *ontological relationship* between text and performance, it, too, suffers from creating a hierarchical structure, giving primacy to the dramatic text. It suffers, further, as a model, as it tells us little about the art form of theatre, itself, as it just explains the *relationship* between theatre's parts (i.e., dramatic text and theatrical performance).

Possible Worlds and "Re-creations"

Later to the game, at least in terms of theatre, the possible worlds thesis was introduced. While not the first to suggest as much, the first book-length study, Thomas Pavel's *Fictional Worlds* (1986) situates the study of literature in the possible worlds thesis, where Pavel equates fictional worlds as possible worlds. While Pavel does not exclude theatre, his book largely ignores it as a unique art form, kind of lumping it together as literature, despite (what we now know are) its generic differences. Irit Degani-Raz (2003, 2005), in two articles, was the first to place the possible worlds thesis specifically in relation to theatre.[5]

Following up on Pavel and Degani-Raz, my book *Analytic Philosophy and the World of the Play* (2017) further develops the possible worlds thesis in relation to theatre, but it complicates it by suggesting that theatre is a "re-creation." Later streamlining the concept of re-creation, also placing it more squarely in D. M. Armstrong's camp (1989), I claim that the world of the play and theatrical characters is composed of, and/or refers to, a cluster of actually existing concrete objects, but they are arranged or recombined in such a way that they do not exist in our world, except as *abstract objects* (Bennett 2021).

While I do not (fully) disagree with my previous claim in Bennett (2017), I do believe that it does fall short when considering some specific instances of theatre and performance and, thus, this view must be further refined and expanded to take into account some outliers (many of which have become mainstream in contemporary theatre). For example, compared to some so-called and so-conceived traditional plays that exist in both dramatic literature and theatrical performance, the following do not fit quite as nicely with the idea of "re-creation": docudrama and/or verbatim theatre, devised theatre, and some one-person shows (which will be explored and explained in Chapter 2, on representation and presentation in the theatre). This is where the idea of positionality explored in the next chapter comes in, by thinking about the relations between/among objects in the theatre.

Recent Debates in Philosophy of Theatre

Apparent in James R. Hamilton's 2019 article "The Philosophy of Theater" in the *Stanford Encyclopedia of Philosophy* and my 2020 article of the same name in *Oxford Bibliographies*, philosophers of theatre have recently explored two prominent lines of inquiry: *mimesis* and *acting*. Long thought to be the artistic activity that most mirrors real life, philosophers of theatre have recently started to question the supposed mimetic quality of theatre as an art form by asking, What sort of artistic activity is theatre? Related to theatre as a mimetic art form are two questions: What is acting, and How is it different from imitation, pretense, action-by-ideal, and so on?

In "What Is Acting?" Yuchen Guo (2022) delineates the necessary and sufficient conditions of acting. Guo suggests that acting is

26 BETWEEN THE LINES

a process of communication between the actor and the audience. For Guo, the two necessary components of acting are that (1) the actor uses his or her own features to represent the features of the character that he or she is playing, and (2) the actor intends to have the audience believe that he or she is *identical* to the character that he or she is portraying. While Guo presents strong argumentation to back up these two necessary conditions of acting, Guo makes an (implied) assumption, and this is where I take issue, that theatrical acting is a mimetic activity. (Guo's article goes well beyond the scope of just *theatrical* acting, but I limit my response to deal only with theatrical acting.) Guo does not specifically call acting a mimetic activity, however; Guo's characterization that acting is the *identical* portrayal of a character certainly can imply that the actor apes or mimes the actions and words of the character. While for millennia, acting was predominantly seen as a mimetic activity, there has been a very recent movement away from this assumption in the emerging field of philosophy of theatre.

I will first outline three contemporary views on acting and, then, three contemporary views on mimesis, to consider the ways in which acting exists in regard to mimesis. Then I will investigate how the reproduction of an identical is problematic in the theatre by raising two objections.

Contemporary Views of Acting

In ways that move past the simplicity of the paradox of doubling in theatrical acting that occupied the minds of theatre theorists in the 1980s to early 2000s (see Olf 1981; States 1983; Saltz 1991; Rayner 1994; Carlson 2003; Zarrilli 2004), theatre theorists and historians and philosophers have explored the complex relationship between subjectivity and the actor. Recent historical studies (Gobert 2013; Camp 2014; Kornhaber 2016; Stern 2017) pave the way for the three most prominent views on acting.

PREVIOUS CONCEPTIONS OF THEATRE   27

Three Contemporary Views of Acting

Guo divides the philosophical approaches to acting into four main accounts:

1. Acting is the interpretation of a script by an actor
2. Theatrical texts are the "ingredients" or "traces" of what actors are to do on stage.
3. Actors are motivated by "as if" desires and conditional beliefs (i.e., "the N&S model").
4. Acting and imagination take two forms *sui generis* (Guo 2021: 1).

While Guo certainly is not wrong to group contemporary views of acting as such, I would like to pose alternative groupings, which more directly engage ideas of theatrical mimesis. Here, I will outline three main contemporary views on acting: (1) acting hides its own behavior; (2) acting is a type of behavior (with some disagreement on what particular type of behavior it is); and (3) acting is a different way of existing.

1. *Acting hides its own behavior.*

Paul Woodruff discusses how acting technique differs from the display of technique in other types of performance. For example, often one marvels at the technique of a virtuoso on the violin or piano, or one is in awe of the perfect technique of a professional golfer's swing. However, in theatrical performance, to be successful, an actor must hide the fact that they are acting. If the audience recognizes the fact that the actor is acting—recognizing the techniques used to act in character—then the illusion of theatre is disrupted. This observation is important from the point of view of categorizing different art forms, specifically how theatre departs from other art forms. While Woodruff fully acknowledges that we tend to only notice acting when it is done poorly, it does seem that an argument can be made that audience members can still recognize technique by way of the

28 BETWEEN THE LINES

negative, in that virtuosity in theatrical acting is equated with *not* noticing the acting.

2. *Acting is a particular type of behavior.*

While there is agreement that acting is *particular type* of human behavior, there is disagreement as to which type of behavior acting is. The three most prominent types of particular behavior are display behavior, performance behavior, and ludic behavior.

a. *Display behavior*

James R. Hamilton develops a theory as to how audiences come to agreement on what they see on stage, as audiences, Hamilton claims, all pick out the same salient features of a performance (2007). Hamilton suggests that acting is a type of display behavior where an actor signals to the audience what to look for (2014, 2017). This is a compelling theory that explains a number of epistemological issues related to the viewing of theatre, yet my hesitation is two-fold: (1) this theory effectively translates into an acting technique that essentially forces actors to replicate *ideals* of gesture and intonation (i.e., creates something of a theory of action-by-ideals), which does not really fall in line with contemporary theories of (teaching) acting (also see Thom 2017), and (2) do audience members from different cultures (and/or socioeconomic environments) agree that the same display of behaviors means the same things?

b. *Performance behavior*

Playing off Ludwig Wittgenstein's notion of "pain behavior," Spencer Golub suggests that performance gives public expression to private experience (Golub 2014). Golub's idea is a powerful one in that Golub recognizes how theatre evokes feelings so intimate and personal, but, as I suggest in Bennett (2021), Golub appears to make an assumption that theatre is also a shared experience among audience members. I claim, instead, that the viewing of a public performance is an individual experience, thinking about how different audience members come with different knowledge to each performance and are, thus, also looking for different information and making different bets as to what is about to happen (2021).

c. *Ludic behavior*

David Saltz has spent his career developing a theory of acting and theatre that suggests that acting is, at base, a ludic behavior, and that theatre is, at base as well, a game (cf., especially Saltz 1991, 2017). Saltz sees theatre as an agreement to play a game between actor and spectator, where everyone agrees to a set of rules to play the game. One key claim is that this agreement is only for the time of the play. That is, actors perform the same actions as the character, but in the context of the rules of the game. Saltz's theory is an all-inclusive theory that touches upon major epistemological and ontological issues surrounding theatre. The only weakness in Saltz's theory that I see, or could pose, is that why does theatre, simply, *feel* so different that other games we play? I do not have an answer to this here, but Saltz assumes something of a uniform audience, which I take some issue with, where (1) the audiences all agree to play the same game and (2) are equally equipped to play the same game (see Bennett 2021).

3. *Acting is existing in a different way.*

Tzachi Zamir claims that, at base, repetition is the key to the acting experience. However, to Zamir, repetition is not simply duplication, but each repetition of an actor allows for the actor to experience something that they already knew "anew" (Zamir 2014: 367). I have, likewise, investigated the idea of "anew" in respect to modern history plays and how the actor and audience must constantly experience that which has already been completed (Bennett 2012). Later, I suggest that the actor is able to relay the sense of "liveness" to the audience by reinterpreting the tense of a dramatic text. As

30 BETWEEN THE LINES

will be re-explored in Chapter 5, I claim that the dramatic text is set up as a two-past mismatched counterfactual (e.g., if it *were* the case that _____ *had been* _____, then it *would have been* the case that _____), but actors change the tenses and combine a one-past counterfactual with a "might" counterfactual (e.g., if it *were* the case that _____, then _____ *might* [*happen*]) to preserve the feelings that something unexpected might happen and keep the sense of possibility alive (Bennett 2017: 86–87).

Contemporary Views of Mimesis

It was not really until the first decade of the twenty-first century that there was a bit of pushback on the metaphor of theatre being a mirror of nature, with an indirect attack on theatrical mimesis by way of nuanced investigations into the concept of "theatricality" and how the term and concept have changed and been used over the millennia. The first sustained examination of the concept of "theatricality" and what it is for something to be "theatrical" (Davis and Postlewait 2004) also brought the related idea of anti-theatricality that can be observed on the modern and contemporary stage (Ackerman and Puchner 2006). Following on the heels of these investigations into theatricality, the first contemporary book-length studies into theatre from a philosophical perspective emerged: James R. Hamilton's *The Art of Theater* (2007) and Paul Woodruff's *The Necessity of Theater* (2008), the latter of which defines the type of theatre he discusses in his book on the value of "mimetic theater."

Three Contemporary Views on Mimesis
There is a spectrum of contemporary views on theatrical mimesis, from (1) theatrical mimesis exists (with the caveat that it is not always used for truth) to (2) theatre is neutral with regard to mimesis to, finally, (3) theatre is not mimetic (but something else).

PREVIOUS CONCEPTIONS OF THEATRE   31

Theatre does, in fact, make use of mimesis, but not always for truth.

The standard model of mimesis in theatre holds that holding up a mirror to nature exposes and reveals the truth about a situation. This is not always the case, though, as Erickson (2009) claims. Erickson points out that William Shakespeare, especially, writes characters who often use mimesis to be untruthful, as, for example, numerous Shakespearean characters act or pretend to be something or someone that they are not.

Theatre is neutral in regard to mimesis.

In regard to the relationship between the theatrical world being presented and the actual world of lived experience, Woodruff claims that "The art of theater is neutral with respect to mimesis" (Woodruff 2017: 111). While Woodruff is more interested in the art of acting, and how performer and audience member should agree that the performance is worth watching to have a success with the art (Woodruff 2017: 110), the question of mimesis is constantly lurking in the background of all theatrical performances. That is, there is an ever-present tension between technique and mimesis, with the latter having to avoid exposing the former (Woodruff 2017: 111).

Theatre does not make use of mimesis, but it makes use of something else.

In *Analytic Philosophy and the World of the Play* (2017), I claim that theatre is not mimetic (i.e., does not reflect the world as would a mirror) and, instead, develop the idea that words, fictional entities, theatrical worlds, and possible worlds are all what I term "re-creation": combinations of actually existing objects arranged in a manner that they do not actually exist except as *abstract objects*. What I attempt to accomplish is two-fold: first, my ontological model for theatre addresses the earlier debates about the relationship between dramatic text and performance (a foundational

32 BETWEEN THE LINES

debate in the field of philosophy of theatre that was chronicled in Hamilton's "The Text-Performance Relationship" in *Philosophy Compass* in 2009). By claiming that both a dramatic text and theatrical performances are re-creations, I attempt to eliminate this dividing line. Further, trying to reinforce this, I put both the text and the performance in the same class of objects, which provides a model for understanding how fictional objects (particularly in the theatre) exist and come into being, providing a seemingly more accurate description of the ontology and ontological status of theatre versus just a simple (though extremely long-lasting) metaphor that theatre is a mirror of nature.

2

The Nature of Theatre

Having just explored previous conceptions of theatre, I want to start this systematic account of theatre with three basic questions about the nature of theatre: Does theatre exist? If so, how does theatre exist? And, finally, what *is* theatre? I can also ask these questions in a different way: What is theatre's ontological status (i.e., does it exist [in some way])? And if theatre does exist, how do we categorize and describe theatre's ontology? This chapter will attempt to answer all these questions.

Fictional entities—such as unicorns, Sherlock Holmes, and Hamlet—have long fascinated philosophers for the ways in which these objects exist (or do not exist) on the margins of reality. As laid out by David Friedell, in his recent article surveying the field in *Philosophy Compass*, the existence or nonexistence of fictional objects has great ramifications to "broader metaphysical issues— including questions about causation, the abstract/concrete distinction, time, vague existence, vague identity, and inadvertent creation" (2021). These are weighty subjects and provide some of the many reasons that philosophers study fictional entities. In some ways, all fictional entities get to the heart of the question, in what way does a fictional entity exist if it is fictional? That is, if Sherlock Homles, or Hamlet, or even a unicorn does not exist, how can we have elaborate conversations about them? And how can we come to some agreement on the nature of each of these fictional characters?

However, philosophers have tended to group theatrical characters—and Hamlet is used quite often—with other fictional characters, such as Sherlock Holmes. The question of the existence of fictional characters becomes even more problematic in the

Between the Lines. Michael Y. Bennett, Oxford University Press. © Oxford University Press 2024.
DOI: 10.1093/9780197691700.003.0003

34   BETWEEN THE LINES

case of theatre, as theatrical characters have a dual existence on the page and the stage. That is, theatrical characters exist as a range of possibilities on the page, while they, *momentarily*, become a single embodied (fictional) reality on any given stage on any given night. This impermanence (or seeming impermanence) is largely why we must raise the question, does theatre exist? Theatre takes fictional characters and places them in a counterfactual situation (i.e., a situation that runs counter to actual facts about our real world) that plays out, repeatedly, day in and day out. So does, or how does, theatre have a material reality due to its momentary existence or its fleeting existence in a moment in time? Given that the performance of theatre centers on real bodies who, for the time of the play, act as fictional characters, let us start by thinking about how a fictional entity exists (if it does)?

Philosophers split into (according to Amie L. Thomasson's important 1999 book, *Fiction and Metaphysics*) five camps surrounding the idea of whether and how a fictional entity exists, with some of these camps drawing on some of the foundational arguments of twentieth-century analytic philosophy. Thomasson posits the following five groups: Meinongians; Possibilists; those who see fictional characters as objects of reference; those who see fictional characters as imaginary objects; and, finally (following her theory), Artifactualists (Thomasson 1999: 5–23). Following Francesco Berto, it is also possible (and, with a bit of hindsight, much simpler) to categorize these groups as *Meinongians* (i.e., fictional names refer to nonexistent objects), *Realists* (i.e., fictional names refer to abstract objects, broadly defined), and *Fictionalists* (i.e., fictional names do not refer).[1] In some respects, these three groups all have differing stances on the same topic, but in some other ways, they are not (fully) at odds with, or really having a debate with one another, as each group has a very different agenda/reason for studying fictional entities.[2]

Relatively recently, philosophers have begun to return to Meinongian theories in the debate surrounding names, reference,

THE NATURE OF THEATRE   35

and fictional entities. In general, however, Meinongian theories are not theories inherently concerned with questions and philosophical problems posed by fiction, but are concerned with the implications that nonexistent objects have on larger questions in ontology and, more broadly, metaphysics.[3]

More recently, fictionalism has asserted that fictional objects simply do not denote actual objects or anything outside of the fictional world of the text. Fictionalists are much more concerned with the philosophy of language and philosophical semantics than ontology and metaphysics. Broadly speaking, fictionalists are not interested in the existence (or nonexistence) of a fictional character; rather, they are concerned with the *truth value* of statements made in fictional works. Fictionalists argue that inherent in fiction is the notion of *pretense*, and they suggest that implied in the statement "Sherlock Holmes is a detective" is the unwritten, but mutually understood prefix that results in "In Arthur Conan Doyle's stories, Sherlock Holmes is a detective"; determining the truth value of the first sentence is problematic, while the second sentence is, simply, true. Fictionalists, thus, eschew the debate between the Meinongians (i.e., fictional characters are *nonexistent*) and the realists (i.e., fictional characters, broadly speaking, *exist* [in some way]) by changing their lines of inquiry to questions of language and semantics.[4]

The realists, broadly speaking, include (1) the possibilists, (2) those who see fictional characters as objects of reference, (3) those who see fictional characters as imaginary objects, and (4) the artifactualists. Realists see—as a general overarching principle—that fictional entities *exist* in some way: most commonly, as *abstract objects*. That is, realists see fictional names as referring to an existent object, even though that object is (generally thought of as) abstract. This group of realists may further be broken down into those who argue that fictional entities are (1) abstract objects (see, most notably, Saul Kripke's *Naming and Necessity*); (2) artifactual objects that exist in their contextual relationships dependent on

36 BETWEEN THE LINES

things that exist (Amie L. Thomasson, most notably, in *Fiction and Metaphysics*); and, finally, (3) *possibilia*, by possibilists, who suggest that fictional entities exist in a "possible world" (most notably, David Lewis, in *On the Plurality of Worlds*). While these theories and their implications for ontology and metaphysics vary widely (without making too much of a blanket statement), realists believe that fictional entities—in some way, shape, or form—exist. Theatrical characters, however, and even more so in their dual existence on the stage and the page, seem to pose an extra layer of complications to the study of fictional entities. Thus far, largely, theatre has been studied as a category of art through philosophical aesthetics. Very few studies have looked at (specifically) theatre ontologically (with the exceptions of Degani-Raz 2003, 2005 and Bennett 2017).

First, I will develop and expand my previous (2017/2021) theory of fictional entities: elucidating types of (created) *abstract objects* that I call *re-created objects* and *re-positioned objects*. From there, I will examine three modes of delivery in the theatre: metaphor, representation, and presentation. I will demonstrate how re-created and/or re-positioned objects are featured in these three theatrical modes.

Re-created Objects

Elsewhere, I have discussed how the word "cat," for example, refers to a cluster of associations with the referent (or, we can say, too, with the *type*): *pet, feline, long-haired, Fluffy, short-haired, whiskers, purr, meow, domesticated, frequent allergen, black spots, yellow spots,* and so on (Bennett 2017, 2021). Instead of a word referring to a specific referent, or to an exact collection or cluster of properties or states, words refer to clusters of separate, individual associations that all together, in full combination, constitute the meaning of a word. However, and here is the key point, every single association need not be present (explicitly or implicitly) to use and/or understand a

THE NATURE OF THEATRE 37

word. And, further, the cluster may contain associations—such as extralingual connections—that are not even a part of the meaning of the word. For example, if I say, "my purring pet," essentially everyone will understand that I am referring to my domesticated feline. I would also equally be able to refer to the same object through the statement "Every time Fluffy meows, I see her whiskers perk up," or the statements "I sneeze whenever I get too close to Fluffy's long-haired coat" or "I get scratched by Fluffy after she licks her paws."

My claim that a word is an abstract object that refers to concrete parts may appear that I advocate for something of a *type*-versus-*token* ontological model of words. If I were to say the word "cat," most would agree that I am referring to a concrete object. Cats do exist (as a *type*). Or at least, Cat_1, Cat_2, Cat_3 . . . exist (as *tokens*). If I were to establish the fact that I own a domesticated feline that I refer to as "Fluffy," and if I were to say, "my cat, Fluffy," I would be creating a more rigid designation for the word "cat" in the context of this proposition. Here, the type/token model explains the ontology of the word "cat" and its relationship to its referent.

However, what if I were with another person, and we both observed a shadow, and if I were to say, "I think *that* is a shadow of a cat," but—in this instance—a cat was not what was casting *that* shadow? I can make the above statement, and my interlocutor and fellow observer could understand what I uttered, because we could examine the shape of the shadow and, given the elements of what makes up a cat (much of what we know both from a dictionary definition and from empirical experience), we can attribute these elements to corresponding elements in that shadow. Of course, too, that shadow would not need to demonstrate all the many things that make cats "cats." This shadow need not, for example, demonstrate that this shadow refers to a domesticated object, or if, further, whether this shadow refers to a cat that may or may not be hypoallergenic, to communicate that this shadow looks like a cat. But clearly, I can say the word "cat" and liken it to a two-dimensional, monotone shape not made by an actual "cat" because, much like

38 BETWEEN THE LINES

that two-dimensional monotone shape, the word "cat" refers, not to a concrete object but to an abstract object. In short, in the case of the word "cat," I suggest that the word "cat" (without more rigidly contextualizing words and/or nonverbal gestures) is an abstract object that, in turn, refers to a cluster of concrete parts. I call abstract objects of this type "re-creations" or "re-created objects."[5]

While I agree with cluster theory's claim that x need not have all the properties in the cluster for "F" to apply to it,[6] re-created objects do not require all of the constituent associations to be a part of the meanings. That is, instead, re-creations can have, as well, an excess of associations (that include connotations beyond what is being referred to and/or denoted). While we can suggest that in this above theory of words, "words" are types (abstract entities), what these words refer to—clusters of associations with the word—are not only tokens (particular instances or occurrences). The reason why fiction (broadly defined) can occur using language is because words refer not only to tokens but also to parts of tokens and parts of a cluster of associations (associations with the type and associations with its constituent tokens).

At base, the intellectual thrust behind fiction is that fictional entities are re-creations that refer to nonexistent recombinations of a particular selection of associations from a cluster of associations (as opposed to states of being or properties).[7] Each one of these associations in the cluster refers, further, either to a particular or to a universal referent (with the referent, further, being either a concrete object or action). Thus, because re-creations refer to clusters of concrete referents and actions which are associated with parts of the whole (i.e., the "whole" being the word, metaphor, fictional entity, fictional world, possible world), this is how, or why, fiction (broadly defined) can occur.

As I claim that fictional entities, fictional worlds, and *even* "possible worlds" are in the same class of objects as words—in that they are all *re-created objects*—there is a hierarchical structure that emerges when considering the relationship among all four of these

THE NATURE OF THEATRE   39

types of *abstract objects*.[8] The building blocks of fictional entities, fictional worlds, and "possible worlds" are words. In short, words build fictional entities, which are then used (among other words) to build fictional worlds, which are then used (among other things) to build "possible worlds." Each layer in this schema is simply more complete and more detailed, but conversely, as the level of detail and completeness increases, the range of "possible worlds" as one moves through and up the schema decreases.

From Abstract Creationism to Re-Creation

As an adherent of it myself, *abstract creationism* believes, as a general overarching principle, that fictional entities are abstract objects that are intentionally created (by humans/artists/writers/etc.). In discussing the creation of fictional objects, Stuart Brock offers three interpretations of the claim John Searle makes that an author creates fictional characters and events by pretending to refer to them. One of the interpretations of Searle's claim is what Brock calls "intended creation by pretense" view (ICP), in which "a fictional object is created whenever (i) an author intends to create a new fictional character and (ii) as a causal consequence of that intention, she pretends to refer to it" (Brock 2010: 356). Brock argues against this as a possible way to understand how fictional objects are created. Brock criticizes David Friedell (2016) for using, what Brock calls, an "indirect response" to defend abstract creationism. Offering a further critique of abstract creationism and ICP, Brock outlines what he ascertains are, at minimum, the questions that an adequate theory of fictional objects should be able to answer (or, at least, provide resources to answer):

Ontology. Are there any fictional objects?
Identity. Under what conditions is a fictional object x identical to a fictional object y?

> **Plentitude.** How abundant is the domain of fictional objects? How many fictional objects are there? (2018: 93)

Brock suggests that Friedell also could have provided, instead of an indirect response to defend abstract creationism, either a direct response to the specific challenges posed by Brock or offer an "ambitious response" that involves a different interpretation of Searle's thesis or an account that is entirely different (2018: 95). While this book does not lay a claim to, specifically, defend ICP, I offer an "ambitious response" as an alternative defense of abstract creationism.

By, instead, modifying our conception of what fictional objects are, in short, I give a defense of abstract creationism that offers answers to the questions, as outlined by Brock, of ontology, identity, and plenitude by developing a claim that—except for rigidly referring proper names—fictional terms, nonfictional terms, and metaphors are all abstract objects. This designation allows for a novel way to examine fictional entities—through an examination of the pieces or parts contained within.

Turning to the questions posed by Brock that could elicit an adequate theory of fictional objects—which include fictional terms and (non-rigidly referring) nonfictional terms—I will answer the questions posed by Brock one at a time:

Ontology. Are there any fictional objects?
Answer: I claim that the issue, here, is, in part, the (somewhat erroneous) idea that these abstract objects are "fictional." Fiction is the opposite of nonfiction. I do not believe that "fiction" is appropriately named, as a "fictional" character contains and refers to a cluster of many concrete objects in this world. Instead, what we think of as "fiction" is, rather, a counterfactual condition. Let me rephrase the question, then, to one we can answer in the affirmative: Are there any abstract objects, or are there any re-creations? Yes.

THE NATURE OF THEATRE   41

Identity. Under what conditions is a fictional object *x* identical to a fictional object *y*?

Answer: The question yields two interpretations. Is the question (1) Under what conditions are Sherlock Holmes and Hamlet identical? or (2) Under what conditions are Sherlock Holmes from one story by Arthur Conan Doyle identical to Sherlock Holmes in another story by Doyle? In regard to (1), Sherlock Holmes and Hamlet are not identical under any conditions, as they are two distinct, abstract objects in two distinct and different fictional worlds. The caveat, however, is that while Sherlock Holmes is an abstract object that, on the whole, is different and distinct from Hamlet, who is also an abstract object, parts of the two fictional objects refer to some of the same concrete aspects: both Sherlock Holmes and Hamlet share traits of a detective (both try to uncover the truth and determine who is the criminal), they are both brilliant, they are both men, and so on. That being said, Sherlock Holmes and Hamlet are composed of recombinations of clusters of associations that ensure that these are two distinct entities: Doyle's Sherlock Holmes lives in Victorian London and William Shakespeare's Hamlet lives in medieval Denmark. These two different fictional worlds, and the two different stories that they are part of, ensure that these are distinct fictional objects.

Regarding (2), Hamlet appears only in Shakespeare's play *The Tragedy of Hamlet, Prince of Denmark*, while Sherlock Holmes appears across a number of short stories by Doyle. This raises another issue, as well: Sherlock Holmes is found in, for example, BBC's television series *Sherlock*, which takes place in contemporary London; Hamlet has been staged in, seemingly, every time period imaginable. While this does bring up a problem about reproducing an identical object, I can also answer the question more simply by indicating whose Sherlock Holmes or Hamlet it is (Shakespeare's Hamlet, Director X's Hamlet, Doyle's Sherlock Holmes, BBC's Sherlock Holmes, etc.).

Plentitude. How abundant is the domain of fictional objects? How many fictional objects are there?

Answer: The domain of fictional objects, or, rather, let us say, abstract objects or re-creations, is as abundant as there are words, and then some (such as combinations of concrete parts that make abstract wholes). An actual limit of combinations might be reached, but for practical purposes, it would be a limit that approaches infinity. We could also suggest, however, that because literature/metaphors can consist of infinitely long texts, infinite re-creations are possible.

Re-creation in Theatre

It is precisely because of this *loose* connection between a word and its cluster of associations that *fiction* (versus a description of reality) can occur. That is, if I say the phrase "Hamlet, Prince of Denmark," I should think that essentially everyone would understand that I am referring to William Shakespeare's fictional/theatrical character, Hamlet. Similar to my above discussion of "cat," I should also equally be able to refer to the same object (i.e., Hamlet) through the statement "Horatio's friend who plots to seek revenge" or phrases "the man who went mad north by northwest" or "the inventor of the mousetrap to catch the conscience of the King." While Hamlet clearly does not exist in our actual world, Hamlet does (I claim) exist as a *re-created object* in that he is a re-creation of concrete objects and actions (e.g., a prince, a Dane, surviving son of a murdered father, seeks revenge, brilliant, creative, etc.). So, then, to whom/what does "Hamlet" refer? I claim that there are really two types of Hamlet (or, really, two types of any theatrical character, to be more explicit): the "*Necessary*-Hamlet" and the "*Possible*-Hamlet."

The "*Necessary*-Hamlet" refers to *one*, and only one, re-created individual in all "possible worlds," who contains the precise specific-and-specified collection of subjects and predicates associated with both the name "Hamlet" and the character Hamlet. The "*Necessary*-Hamlet" does not, and cannot, exist except as an abstract object, specifically as a *re-created object* (unless somehow Hamlet from Shakespeare's *Hamlet* could appear and come to life as in Pirandello's play). This Hamlet is a *necessarily* true Hamlet. But, again, this *Necessary*-Hamlet cannot exist except as an abstract object.

The "*Possible*-Hamlet" refers, however, to a *range* of re-created individuals, each of whom can contain a wide range of concrete properties and actions that are possibly associated with both the name "Hamlet" and the character Hamlet. This *Possible*-Hamlet refers, then, to many re-created individuals in different "possible worlds," who can each claim the possibility of being Hamlet. However, none of these *Possible*-Hamlets exist in every "possible world." The presumption about the *Possible*-Hamlets is that they each contain the same *kernel of Hamlet* but also contain many other possible concrete objects and actions that are not specific to or specified by the *Necessary*-Hamlet.

As falling under the purview of re-creation, classifying theatrical characters as *re-created objects* takes into account, even explains, the inherent imprecision of description and reference in names of fictional entities. That is, a *re-created object* contains an entire *range* of re-creations. For example, in theatre, the dramatic text specifies/limits the *range of re-creations* possible for a given theatrical character. That is, the dramatic text specifies/limits the range of who can possibly be (and who cannot possibly be) the said theatrical character in question. The performance, however, embodies a *single re-creation* of that theatrical character. Therefore, a dramatic text contains *all* of the possible re-creations of an individual (i.e., theatrical character); in every performance, a singular re-creation of an individual (i.e., theatrical character) is embodied.

44 BETWEEN THE LINES

Re-positioned Objects

Instead of looking just at objects and what these objects are, refer to, and/or are composed of (i.e., from the *words, sounds, bodies, images,* and *objects* typical of other art forms mentioned in the Introduction), in this book, I also want to think about the relationships among objects and/or how objects are *re-positioned* with/against each other.[9] That is, theatre does not only come into being by re-creating nonexistent objects (i.e., by combining concrete objects and actions in such a way that they do not actually exist). Sometimes it also comes into being by looking at existent objects from different vantage points, by re-positioning objects, either alone or in relation to other objects. Here, I am using the idea/concept of re-positioning not as a technical term, but merely using its commonsense notion that if you change the position of an object or an idea, either alone or in relation to something else, that it can be viewed differently. Theatre is not just fiction-world creating through words but through objects as well. So the ontological issue becomes not only whether some fictional character exists but whether some fictional object exists in virtue of the real-world object it tracks. In other words, what is the relationship between the fictional and nonfictional objects in theatre?

By examining the blank spaces of theatre, this book is able to get to the very heart of how *the real* and *the imaginary* interact in theatre. This topic has been explored at great length by the many who look at theatre from a phenomenological perspective, but the ability to describe the relationship of the real to the imaginary in theatre has remained quite elusive and has been quite hard to pin down in theatre and performance studies, thus far. I claim that theatre *re-creates* and/or *re-positions* objects that exist in our world to create (or "re-create") different and/or new *relations* among its constituent pieces, using one, or more than one, of the following figurative expressions: (1) metaphorical, (2) representational, and (3) presentational.

THE NATURE OF THEATRE 45

Figurative Expressions

Metaphor in the Theatre

One of the most fundamental devices in the arts is metaphor. Along with simile and allegory, metaphor forms the backbone of fiction, broadly conceived. Here, I will examine how metaphor has been conceived and also how we can better conceive metaphor to more accurately describe what is happening in theatre.

I. A. Richards's definition of metaphor still holds much sway in philosophical semantics and in philosophical aesthetics: a known object/concept, called the *vehicle* (also known as the secondary subject), is used to illuminate an unknown object/concept, called the *tenor* (also known as the primary subject).[10] This definition—which is even more simply stated that a metaphor is a *likening* between two objects/concepts—is used to form the base of our understanding surrounding metaphor. However, metaphor (or literature, which can be argued to be an extended metaphor) generally helps us *understand* (our world, or something in it); this is different than I. A. Richards's idea of *tenor* and *subject*, which generally attempts to *describe* (our world, or something in it) by using the attributes of the vehicle to describe the tenor.

Two figures of speech—metonymy and synecdoche—are intimately related to metaphor, as conceived by Richards. Metonymy is a figure of speech where something adjacent or contiguous replaces the original. That is, metonymies such as "The Crown" or "The White House" replace, respectively, the King and/or Queen and/or their kingdom or the President of the United States of America and/or the Office of the President. Synecdoche is another figure of speech where a part replaces the whole, or the whole replaces a part. Synecdoches such as "wheels," "heads," and "ABCs" are used in place of a car, cows as a part of a herd of cattle, and the alphabet. Both of these figures of speech are metaphorical, but in a large sense, when presented alone, they are likenings that are vehicles to describe tenors.

46   BETWEEN THE LINES

Largely unbeknownst to most philosophers, linguists, and even literary critics, however, a large body of work on the study of metaphor has been done, in fact, by biblical scholars. The study of metaphor relates to the primacy of "parables," both in the *Hebrew Bible* (i.e., *meshalim*, plural, or *mashal*, singular, is the Hebrew word to describe a wide variety of literary forms, one of which is "parable"[11]), and, even more so, in *The New Testament* with the parables of Jesus (as about 40 percent of the words spoken by Jesus are done so in the form of parables). The history of understanding parables is tied up with *allegory*, the latter of which is a fictional text that refers, with *one-to-one correspondence*, to something outside of the text. For example, *Animal Farm* is an allegory *of* communism, or *The Crucible* is an allegory *of* McCarthyism, or "The Prodigal Son" is an allegory *of* the Christian worldview that God welcomes back sinners who ask for forgiveness (where the father refers to God and the son refers to human-as-sinner). That is, this idea of a likening in metaphor—especially when the phrases are used, *this is a metaphor for*, or *this is a metaphor of*—really has its roots in allegory and allegorical readings. The idea of metaphor *for* or metaphor *of* is similar to many *pragmatic twist accounts* of metaphor, where the speaker or writer says one thing and something else is meant. I contend that the previous iteration of metaphor is closer to allegory or analogy, as it requires a likening or is referring to an object outside of itself.

While allegorical readings of the parables of Jesus may be familiar to and still heard by, say, churchgoers to this day, biblical scholars, and particularly *New Testament* scholars have, for decades, taken the position that, at base, a parable is a metaphor. Sallie McFague (1975) says that the meaning of the parable is contained within the story itself, but it is not limited by the story: "A parable is an extended metaphor. A parable is not an allegory, where the meaning is extrinsic to the story. . . . Rather, as an extended metaphor, the meaning is found only within the story itself although it is not exhausted by that story" (1975: 13). Both a parable and/or metaphor are *irreducible*, in that a metaphor is

THE NATURE OF THEATRE   47

only itself and cannot be reduced or transposed into, or onto, anything else other than itself: as C. H. Dodd says, "any attempt to paraphrase its meaning is both less clear and less forcible than the saying as it stands" (1965: 23).[12] In this manner, parables and/or metaphors are explained adequately by *brute force accounts*, most notably by Donald Davidson (1978). These brute force accounts are, specifically, however, maintained to explain the *meaning* or *truth* of a metaphor, and not the, per se, ontology or ontological status of metaphor.[13] Again, if a metaphor referred, or were likened, to a referent(s) outside of the text, then it becomes an allegory and/or an analogy. However, literature—broadly defined to include fiction, drama (and theatre), and poetry—works precisely because there is *no specific* referent or likening. As such, most of traditional, text-based theatre works through metaphor.

As a means to demonstrate, as I do in *Analytic Philosophy and the World of the Play*, take Maurice Valency (1966) and his classic book on modern drama as an example. Besides Valency's ability to categorize and compare drama from the Greeks through his present, Valency writes beautifully, explicating metaphors with ease. Valency's talent is no more on display than in his discussion of Henrik Ibsen's *The Master Builder*, from where he gets half of the title for his book, *The Flower and the Castle*. Ibsen's play is about Solness, a "master builder" (i.e., an architect), who is past the prime of a successful career and, fearing being replaced by the younger generation, wants to build a "castle in the air," a house with a spire taller than any church:

> It is one thing to aspire, quite another to attain the heights of one's aspiration. No artist is able to realize in life the ideal he expresses in art. The disparity between what a man says and what he does is the measure of the man, not the artist. Moreover, the attempt to surmount in reality the peak of one's fancy may prove to be a perilous business for one not properly equipped for the asperities of the ascent. (Valency 1966: 209)

48   BETWEEN THE LINES

In explicating Ibsen's elegant metaphors (i.e., "master builder" and "castle in the air"), Valency uses two objects (i.e., "spire" and "architect") that come directly from the plot of the play. First, he uses the "spire" of the house in the sense of the somewhat-antiquated verb form, "spire," to get to "aspire": "spire, *v.* 3. To rise or shoot up into a spire or spire-shaped form; to rise or extend to a height in the manner of a spire; to mount or soar aloft" (*OED*), which is not the direct root of the word "aspire," but both are etymologically related. Most obviously, and much more likely the reason Valency chose the word, the verb "aspire" literally contains the word "spire." From the definition of the verb "aspire," Valency draws upon the dictionary definition of these words and ideas:

aspire, *v.* 1. to seek to attain or accomplish a particular goal
    2. ascend, soar

Valency essentially just rewrites the first definition of "aspire" in the first sentence of the above passage, "to attain the heights of one's aspiration," using the cognate of "aspire" (i.e., "aspiration"—"3 *a*: a strong desire to achieve something high or great") to connote both ideas of "height" (related to the "great" height of the spire) and of a "goal." In Valency's use of the object, "architect" ("1: a person who designs buildings and advises in their construction"), he is not using exactly the above dictionary definition, but develops his own extended metaphor, from what an "architect" literally does: that is, an architect creates a design, a blueprint, that is used, later, to turn the architect's idea into a material reality. From this very literal description of an architect, Valency uses, this time in a more creative way, the idea of "design" to discuss the difference between an "ideal" design (i.e., "the peak of one's fancy") and the "disparity" between that "ideal" and the idea of the verbs, "aspire" and "spire" (i.e., "attempt to surmount in reality the peak of one's fancy"), and the "reality" ("No artist is able to realize in life the ideal he expresses in art"). Finally, Valency returns to the word "ascent"—a cognate

THE NATURE OF THEATRE   49

of one of the above definitions of "aspire"—to demonstrate the "measure" of this "disparity" between the creation of an "ideal" and its existence in "reality."

Valency describes that while, from a "practical viewpoint," the necessary "ability to climb buildings with a wreath in his hand" is "bizarre," very importantly, Valency demonstrates that "as metaphors they are transparent." I use Valency's passage as a dual example of how extended metaphor (i.e., fiction/literature, broadly defined) is "transparent" in the ways in which it is both created (or, rather, re-created), and understood, by its unique collection of concrete referents selected from a cluster of associations. These associations, both inherent in the word/referent but also sometimes only associated with, are arranged (or recombined) in such a manner (and with a general incompleteness) that Solness and the world of *The Master Builder* do not actually exist, except as a re-creation that has ontological status as an abstract object. As I have used the example of *The Master Builder*, metaphor serves as the base of the vast majority of pieces of traditional text-based theatre.

Representation in the Theatre

In *Painting as Art*, Richard Wollheim develops a theory of "seeing in" versus "seeing as." When one *sees* x *as* y, one observes x and y in the same ontological category (e.g., the painting of a horse as a horse). In a sense, "seeing as" is similar to what Nelson Goodman, in *Languages of Art*, suggests happens in pictures, where—like in language—representations *refer* (and have a corresponding grammar of syntactic and semantic rules). However, to return to Wollheim, in art (particularly painting), one may *see* y *in* x (e.g., horror in an abstract painting, majesty in a painted cloud, a call for democratic ideals in a painting of farmworkers, etc.). In this respect, Roger Scruton, in his book *Art and Imagination*, discusses

50 BETWEEN THE LINES

how art has a "double intentionality," where an experience is both directed at the work of art and also what is taken away from it.[14]

John Dilworth, in *American Philosophical Quarterly* and the *Journal of Aesthetics and Art Criticism*, suggests that the notion of "representation" helps explain the nature of both dramatic text and theatrical performance, where a play is a *type* and performance is a *token* of that type. Dilworth's discussion of *representation* in the theatre revives the topic of "representation" that has received ample attention as it (more generally) relates to art and aesthetics. Nelson Goodman's *Languages of Art* (1968), Richard Wollheim's *Art and Its Objects* (1968), and Kendall L. Walton's *Mimesis as Make-Believe* (1990) are seminal books in philosophical aesthetics that make foundational arguments about the centrality of representation in understanding art.

But how does representation work in the theatre? In traditional text-based theatre, as in the section above on metaphor, much of theatre is neither entirely the display of the real nor the display of the purely fictional. Metaphor, again, works via re-creation. Representation, then, generally falls into the work of docudrama and/or verbatim theatre, as it is the *re*-presentation of an original object or action. In so many words, representation is a once-removed, but re-positioned object or action, in that docudrama and/or verbatim theatre *re*-present an actual object or action, without seeing or experiencing that actual object or action directly, but mediated through the actors on stage.

Two of the most famous examples of docudrama and/or verbatim theatre are *The Laramie Project* and the theatrical works of Anna Deveare-Smith. *The Laramie Project* is a woven tapestry of words spoken by people related to the homophobic attack and horrific murder of Matthew Shepard in Laramie, Wyoming. The production creates a narrative by actors who speak the words of the people they interviewed. This layering of actual transcripts shows how many people were touched and still touched by the death of Shepard. The actors, in a broad sense, re-present the

THE NATURE OF THEATRE   51

voices and stories of the actual people involved. Anna Deveare-Smith similarly interviews people surrounding a usually tumultuous event in recent history and then performs all of the people herself. This creates a sense that there is a common humanity. All of the people involved or commenting upon these events are mediated through the body and voice of Deveare-Smith. This, similarly, is a once-removed presentation that represents the people involved.

Presentation in the Theatre

To "present" an object or action means "to introduce" that object/action, "bring[ing]. . . into the presence of" something/someone (*OED*). There is something of a sense of newness about presentation; like the television series *Alfred Hitchcock Presents* (1955–1965), what follows is a never-before-seen story. That is, to "present" is also "to show, exhibit, display" (*OED*), with "exhibit" containing the idea of the other two, "to submit or expose to view; to show, to display" (*OED*). These exhibits are not, importantly, re-creations or re-presentations, but are simply showing/telling something about objects and/or actions.

Presentation is when a piece of theatre (1) makes no (or at least very little) attempt to either re-create a so-called fictional object or even an entire fictional world, or (2) does not work via representation to re-position objects in a manner not previously seen before. Theatrical presentation is a theatrical show (per se). Presentation is (in general) the mode of performance art and one-person shows. When Guillermo-Gomez Peña and Coco Fusco sat in a cage as Amerindians in front of museums around the world, they presented themselves as actually existing objects (despite being, rather, re-creations). Karen Finley's scatological shows did not summon up a world or a character, but her flesh and feces presented objects in a newly re-positioned light.

52 BETWEEN THE LINES

Re-creation Playing out on Stage

My notion of "re-creation" in theatre, then, poses a direct challenge to Guo's necessary conditions of theatrical acting (as outlined in Chapter 1). Guo summarizes the necessary conditions in the following expression:

> The actor S portrays a character C *iff* S intends audiences to imagine that S is identical with C, and S represents her own features as the features that C would have (C is either a different individual or the actor herself at a different time). (2021)

Guo argues that the audience (1) is to imagine that actor S is identical with character C because that is how actor S intends to portray character C, and (2) sees S as having the features that C would have.

But what happens when we do not assume that actor S intends audiences to imagine that S is *identical* with C? I have an answer for this:

> by changing the medium [from dramatic text to theatrical performance], regardless of any edits or changes to the original dramatic text, the characters and conditions in the text, once enacted, no longer refer to the range of characters and conditions that are possible in the text. The fixing of a single "possible world" through enacting it in a theatrical production practically ensures that the enacted text is/has to be different than the dramatic text, as the dramatic text also contains other "possible worlds" that may be entirely different than this singled out and fixed, enacted "possible world." (Bennett 2017: 66)

By changing the medium from dramatic text to theatrical performance, a single embodiment of a character cannot be identical to the textual character, as the textual character embodies a range of possibilities, whereas a single embodied character, by actor S, can only embody one possible character from within a range of possible characters. I give an example of this:

> the dramatic text *Waiting for Godot* contains a range of "possible worlds": from Bert Lahr, E. G. Marshall, and Kurt Kasznar's 1956 *Godot* to Nathan Lane, Bill Irwin, and John Goodman's 2009 *Godot*. Both the 1956 *Godot* and the latter 2009 *Godot* are *contained in* Beckett's dramatic text of *Godot*. For example, Lahr's Estragon—"who seems to stand for all of the stumbling, bewildered people of the earth who go on living without knowing why"—is clearly different than Lane's Estragon—"a loveable, loud buffoon, whose physical gestures and movement were demonstrative and sure," where "Estragon's joy of life and folly seemed to comfort Vladimir." (Bennett 2017: 66–67)

In this above case, the audience or audiences have to imagine that this is actor S's character C, or this is actor T's character C (to use Guo's terminology).

But, further, Guo ignores the theatrical practice of cross-casting, as sometimes audiences learn more about a character and its play by not trying to imagine the actor as identical with the character. As we will explore in more detail in Part II of this book, changing the extrinsic property of the gender of the character, by the casting of men to portray Lady Bracknell in Oscar Wilde's *The Importance of Being Earnest* (1895), helps not just the audience but also scholars and future audiences better understand the intrinsic nature of Lady Bracknell. In this case, the audience clearly will not identify the male actor portraying Lady Bracknell as identical to the character, Lady Bracknell, in Wilde's dramatic text.

So what now? If Guo's reliance on reproducing an identical to explain the necessary and sufficient conditions of theatrical acting falls short, via some of my claims and arguments, then does "re-creation" offer an alternative path forward to understand the necessary and sufficient conditions of acting? I am not sure. My goal has

54 BETWEEN THE LINES

been to describe the ontological status of both theatrical characters and the theatre. Guo is attempting to develop a theory of acting. While it is possible that "re-creation" may offer its own solution to outline the necessary and sufficient conditions of theatrical acting, it feels like a stretch, at this precise moment, to base a theory of theatrical acting off of my ontological claims. I do think, though, that both the rejection of theatrical mimesis and the objections raised, indirectly, by my work are important enough to note and should be considered when developing future theories of theatrical acting.

3

The Nature of Viewing Theatre

No man ever steps in the same river twice, for it is not the same river, and he is not the same man.

—Heraclitus

Now that I have outlined and explicated my claims as to what theatre *is*, the question becomes, How do we go about *viewing* theatrical objects? That is, I have claimed that theatre is composed of, and refers to, a group of abstract objects that I call re-created objects and re-positioned objects that are relayed through metaphor, representation, and presentation. So how do we, as both readers and/or audience members, make sense of those objects that we see in the theatre? While viewing a performance may seem like a straightforward activity, how is it that we walk away from viewing the same event with different experiences?

I have previously relayed the parable "The Blind Men and the Elephant" to demonstrate some of the epistemological problems of viewing a performance. In the generic version of this parable, each blind man touches a different part of an elephant and, thus, has a much different view (or understanding) of what an elephant is. This is analogous to what happens in the theatre, not just over the course of a single viewing or performance, but over the course of the life of a piece of theatre. The question must be asked like this: How do audience members come to different understandings and have different experiences when all (seemingly) experience the same observational data when watching a performance?

Unlike, say, knowledge about who is playing character Y, while all the following are understood based upon the same concrete events,

Between the Lines. Michael Y. Bennett, Oxford University Press. © Oxford University Press 2024.
DOI: 10.1093/9780197691700.003.0004

56 BETWEEN THE LINES

most of these other things that we usually think of as knowledge of a performance, instead, fall into the realm of, more broadly, *justified belief*: intonation of spoken lines (e.g., Was the line "whispered" or "murmured audibly"?); feelings of the characters that the actors project (e.g., Was the character "angry" or "incensed"?); mood created by the lighting design (e.g., Was the lighting projecting a "bleak" or a "dark" mood?); and, among many other examples, gesture (e.g., Was the arm "thrusted" or "whipped out"?). The questions raised by these parenthetical examples of justified beliefs about a performance event are two-fold: (1) Are these examples of *justified beliefs* or examples of *justified true beliefs*?[1] and (2) Can two or more people hold different justified true beliefs about the same event? In short, if someone holds a justified belief that the lighting of a particular performance was "bleak" and another holds a justified belief that the lighting of the same performance was "dark," can/do they both simultaneously hold justified true beliefs about the lighting design of this same performance event (even though their beliefs are different)?

I am not sure that this book has precise answers to these two specific questions, but these questions do seem to muddy the waters between observational data and the interpretation of that observational data. That is, if one "thrusted" an arm or "whipped out" an arm, is there an observational difference between the two actions? Can an arm be straightened quickly in two different ways: a way that it is "thrusted" versus a way that it is "whipped out"? And could, in isolating the movement of the arm, anyone perceive the difference between those two, and/or is there any difference between the two? (Try the following yourself as you read this: try to "thrust" your arm out and then try to "whip out" your arm. Is there any difference, and/or could an outside observer notice a difference between those two movements? [Conceptually, I can fully understand the two movements as different and distinct, but I, personally, cannot discern any difference of feel or of look when I try to do this myself.]) Or is merely the circumstances of

THE NATURE OF VIEWING THEATRE   57

the viewer as to why one viewer holds that it was "thrusted" and another holds that it was "whipped out"? That is, if an arm is extended quickly, can it not both be true that it was "thrusted" and/ or "whipped out"? Therefore, can it not also be the case that both viewers hold two different justified true beliefs about the same observational data?

Projecting "Degrees of Belief"

The purpose of relaying the parable "The Blind Men and the Elephant" was to demonstrate how understanding is both subjective and not uniform in an audience, and thus, viewing performance, while a public event, may not be a shared experience. But what happens if we repeat the "Blind Men and the Elephant" scenario over and over again with changing and/or rotating participants? That is, some blind men may be confronting one part of the elephant for the first time, while others may be revisiting the same part of the elephant or experiencing a different part of the elephant than they have experienced before.

Whether it is the first time one of these blind men is touching the elephant or the tenth time, each additional stroke of the elephant yields additional information for each blind man, be it new information or confirmation and/or rejection of previous knowledge/justified beliefs/beliefs. As a group, considering the blind men as a whole, all of these additional pieces of information from the blind men with different experiences yield a more complete understanding of an elephant after consulting with one another and past blind men who also felt the same elephant. It is one thing to try to understand the experience after the event and with the help of others (though with different degrees of belief). However, what happens during the experience of the event? How does understanding change and/or become more accurate with added information through the passage of time? If we take this same group of

58 BETWEEN THE LINES

blind men, each additional stroke gives more clues as to what the future strokes of the elephant might be like.

To return to our arm that is "thrusted" or "whipped out," would it not be the case that the first time you tried this experiment, you would feel and observe no difference? But is it possible that with practice, a highly skilled mover—a professional dancer, for example—could do these two movements, and maybe a professional dance critic, for example, could see the difference? I cannot tell the difference between a pianist at a house of worship playing a piece versus a true virtuoso playing the same material, just as I cannot hear the difference between when I hit a single key on a piano versus when my aunt, a former professional, hits a single note, versus when a true world-class virtuoso hits a single key. I cannot discern a difference at all, but my aunt certainly can. Therefore, just like our blind men touching the elephant, the *circumstances* matter.

Without trying to bring up questions of *authority*, as that further muddies the waters, this raises another prospect: *accuracy*.[2] Would it not, *likely*, be the case that the blind man touching the elephant for the one hundredth time might be more *accurate* about the elephant than the first time one of our blind men ever touches an elephant? (A parallel, of course, is that my aunt will hear things and nuances in a piano performance that I would never even hear and/or notice.) If I am a complete newbie to something, I may not know enough to know that I do not know that others can know more. But with increased exposure, I both learn increasingly that I know less and others can know more. Therefore, part of the equation is whether one knows enough to know whether their own beliefs based upon their own observations are justified or not. The other part, however, is to what degree can they be justified or certain?

The implication here is that there remains the following question when there is disagreement: Is knowledge that is received by observational data (1) a matter of objectivity, which some understand and some misunderstand? or (2) a matter that is, ultimately, of interpretation? I am not suggesting that a concrete reality does

THE NATURE OF VIEWING THEATRE   59

not exist, but there is the question as to whether, given all of our differing circumstances, we can ever have the same knowledge of the same concrete reality or, related and more relevant to this book, have the same experience of the same concrete reality. I am not sure I am fully prepared in this book to make a definitive assertion one way or the other, but I hope that the case of theatre and performance will help us get to a better place—into a better position and circumstance—in which to answer this fundamental question.

Again, as I have claimed that much of what we view at a performance event is based upon, not only knowledge, but beliefs and, importantly, justified beliefs and justified true beliefs, this parable, "The Blind Men and the Elephant," is quite relevant to theatre and performance because the principles of vagueness are inherent in performance (especially in the case of text-based theatre).[3] There are *constants* (e.g., the lines laid out in the dramatic text) and *variables* (e.g., the variety of performance choices) that are continually *projected* forward. Both the performers and the viewers project their beliefs (of various degrees of certainty) to be more certain of what is before them (with objects that do not present themselves as black-and-white, true-or-false, objective facts).

Performance and Bayesian Epistemology

Once we introduce this idea of *projecting variables* (or projecting beliefs), to understand concrete objects and/or actions, we fall into the realm discussing the "probability calculus," central to Bayesian statistics (it sounds utterly daunting, and it *can* be *extremely* technical, but the basic concepts, without the need for any math, are quite simple). Developed out of a famous mathematical theorem about probability by Reverend Thomas Bayes (1701–1761), Bayesian statistics and probability calculus are based upon the concept of *betting behavior*, which is "the inclination to accept and reject bets according to our degrees of belief."[4] By extending this idea

60 BETWEEN THE LINES

to philosophy, in the field of "Bayesian epistemology,"[5] the "proba-bility calculus is especially suited to represent degrees of belief (or *credences*) and to deal with questions of belief change, confirma-tion, evidence, justification, and coherence."[6] This idea of meas-uring one's betting behavior based upon one's "degrees of belief" is especially relevant to performance since, as I have suggested that performance *projects a counterfactual* (versus a *fact*), Bayesian ideas about probability and the conditions of viewing become important here because the audience is constantly being exposed new infor-mation, and while knowledge changes, so, too, does one's degrees of belief. However, further, there must remain opposing senses and/ or feelings of *plausibility* and of *surprise*. That is, as the performance goes on, the viewer should continually possess the belief that some-thing *might* or *could* happen,[7] or else there is generally little pleasure in the viewing process if the viewer's expectations of what is going to happen are constantly met (i.e., the performance becomes *pre-dictable*). In short, without the need to get into the weeds of logic and mathematics, engaging with general insights from Bayesian epistemology helps explain why viewers have different experiences while viewing the same observational data.

For simple purposes of reference, in order to explain the fundamentals of the Bayesian "probability calculus," I use the following formula (based upon the "Simple Principle of Conditionalization"): $P_{new}(A) = P(A \mid E)$. While the formula can look rather complex, it is a generally simple idea that can be used to quantify one's new degree of certainty about an object or event when new information is presented that affects one's prior de-gree of certainty about an object or event. Here, P represents the "*probability corresponding to S's degree of belief.*" Simply, P means that a person (i.e., S) believes that A will occur [0–100] percent of the time. Therefore, let us say that A is *the occurrence that at least one character dies in the final scene* of a particular Shakespearean tragedy that S has not seen. We could say that for S—who, let us say, is a college-educated theatre or English major graduate—that his

THE NATURE OF VIEWING THEATRE   61

or her $P(A)$ is 90 percent (or, technically, .90). In plain English, that means that S believes with a 90 percent degree of belief of A, or this person has a 90 percent degree of belief that at least one character will die in the final scene of this particular Shakespearean play that he or she has not seen. Let us say, further, that as the play goes along, S encounters some new information that is relevant to this person's $P(A)$, which means new information that affects this person's degree of belief that at least one character will die in the final scene of this play. We call this new information E. At the moment that this new information is revealed, we can calculate a new P (i.e., $P\mathit{new}$), where, given E, S believes that A will occur a new percent of the time. In short, S believes that (now) after learning E, that A will occur ___ percent of the time. Stated another way, after learning E, S (now) believes with ___ percent degree of belief that A will occur.

This general concept from Bayesian epistemology helps explain differences in the viewing experience for different members of an audience. For example, maybe a college-educated theatre or English major might have a $P(A)$ of 90 percent, referring to the fact that in a Shakespearean tragedy not seen before that this person believes that there is a 90 percent chance that at least one character will die at the end of the play. However, let us say another viewer in the same audience is a fourteen-year-old freshman in high school and this is the first Shakespeare play they have ever read or seen. Not only would the fourteen-year-old's sense of the probability (i.e., P) vary of what will transpire, the very notion of what can or cannot, or might or might not, transpire (i.e., A), will vary greatly, as well. Now, compare this to, say, a Shakespearean scholar or actor, who has read and seen the play (or maybe acted in this play) a number of times. Their sense of probability (i.e., P) of what will transpire (i.e., A) will be quite different, both their assuredness and what facts they are looking for. That is, this Shakespearean scholar or actor is not looking for the same A as our college-educated English or theatre major, the "occurrence that one character dies at the end of the play," but their A, the occurrence or object they are looking for, might be how this particular production, and the actors within, handle a particular scene, in terms of, say, how seriously or humorously a few lines are acted.

This above example about a high school freshman and a Shakespearean actor or scholar both watching the same play highlights an important issue: *What is the relationship between receiving common data and having the same experience?* In *Subjective, Intersubjective, Objective* (2001), Donald Davidson introduces the concept of *triangulation* to epistemology in situations where two or more creatures interpret both the world and each other simultaneously, where "each creature learns to correlate the reactions of other creatures with changes or objects in the world to which it also reacts."[8] For Davidson, the "shared perceptual stimulus" of two or more minds reacting to the world yields a "triangular set of relations."[9] Building off Davidson's ideas about triangulation, I want to suggest that the more minds/observers there are reacting to the same object, the less the effect of parallax: the more observers, the more understandings can be *superimposed* on one another.[10] Essentially, the more superimpositions that come from more viewers from many and different angles, the more accurate the viewing (and think of Google Earth as a *world*-ly example of this). To this conception of superimposing, we can add the rationale from Bayesian epistemology for the *variety-of-evidence thesis* in thinking about confirmation theory—"the more varied the evidence is, the better"—and also the fact that the act of superimposing, like Bayesian epistemology, takes into account the source of knowledge/belief, being able "to model the effect of combining the testimony of several witnesses."[11] To be clear, while triangulation happens mostly after performance, that is not to say that Bayes's theory stops at the end of a theatrical production and, then, triangulation takes over: Bayes's theory continues to apply well after the time of a theatrical production. That is, making use of triangulation, one continues to update their knowledge of the play, as well as their experiences, even after the theatrical production concludes.

THE NATURE OF VIEWING THEATRE   63

On a smaller scale (than Google Earth) to demonstrate my ideas about triangulating knowledge, I would like to make a slight adjustment to the end of Edmund L. Gettier's famous example, come to be known as the "Gettier Problem,"[12] to address the idea that some things present themselves as internally illogical, but are perfectly logical externally:

> When Smith makes his assertion that the man with ten coins in his pocket will get the job, Smith—unbeknownst to himself—does indeed have ten coins in his pocket. In the next few proceeding hours, after purchasing a snack and lunch, however, Smith spends the coins that were in his pocket, unaware of how many he had in his pocket in the first place. After lunch, Smith gets awarded the job. His assessment that the man with ten coins will get the job appears to be false.

Internally there is a contradiction; externally it is logical. With overlapping experience and knowledge from both the snack vendor and the lunch vendor—while Smith was justified in his belief that the man with ten coins in his pocket would get the job and did not know his assertion was true—Smith can learn that his original assertion was true, and that he was justified in believing it, even though that original assertion presented itself as false. The approach to external truth, seemingly illogical, now based upon the internal contradiction, can be approached by triangulating the experiences of Smith, the snack vendor, and the vendor at lunch. Much in the same way, our thought experiment theatre spectators—A, B, and C—can learn about the performance by triangulating their three experiences.

Following the observation about the difficulty of taking in *all* of a play, the only remaining path left to approach an understanding of the totality of performance lays in the fact that the more contexts—personal and group—that can be overlaid on top of one another by triangulation, the smaller the error from personal, and group, parallax. With its corresponding infinitesimally larger units and

64 BETWEEN THE LINES

infinitesimally smaller units, the concept of infinity ensures that error from parallax is impossible to overcome (e.g., something like Zeno's paradox of Achilles and the Tortoise). For clarity, I am not using "parallax" in the same way as Slavoj Žižek's Lacanian use of it in his book *The Parallax View*. Instead, I am invoking the literal use of the term as it pertains to (visual) perception (i.e., experiencing the world from different circumstances or positions). Different circumstances inherently allow some direct lines of experience, indirect lines of experience, and blocked lines of experience. Due to the resulting parallax—with no God-like observer to work to mesh these views the way that our brain, via stereopsis, makes the visual parallax into one clear image—there must be interpersonal, interpersonal and group, and intergroup stereopsis by way of layering contexts and evaluating the displacement, the alignment, and/or error to gain knowledge about the object being viewed.

In light of epistemic concerns about other minds, using theatre and performance as case studies demonstrates that the relationship among justified belief, knowledge, and truth (to think back to the "Gettier Problem") is a product of the overlap of personal and group contexts and circumstances.[13] The case of theatre and performance, then, furthers the conclusion that objective facts are more fully revealed *after* the viewing. In its totality, a performance event is (1) not quite an exact time-place-space-defined event, (2) too complex to observe all aspects of the event, and (3) based on different subjective understandings of the event based on different subjective experiences of the individual spectators. Triangulation from individual spectators and groups, therefore, is necessary to lessen the parallax created by these three above-mentioned factors.

Theatre as a *Living* Idea

Viewing performance blurs the line between private/individual and public/shared experiences, in part, because *performance lives.*

THE NATURE OF VIEWING THEATRE   65

As one calls the Constitution of the United States a "living document," one can also argue that *performance is a living idea of embodied artistic expression*. Performance is made up of a series of *concrete* objects and events that can only, however, be understood in its entirety as an *abstract object*. While the essential composition remains the same—if delineated and bounded by a dramatic text—the changing parts and participants of performance constantly change. Those same bounds can change shape, shade, color, and intensity based upon how the performance participants understand the shape, shade, color, and intensity of the text. In turn, this affects how we understand the shape, shade, color, and intensity of the text. A piece of performance, then, is a living idea that develops both within and changes the perceivable boundaries delineated by the text. The ever-changing parts and participants of performance across time and place are precisely what reveal the limits but also the many different shapes, shades, colors, and levels of intensity that can (or cannot) exist within the malleable container that houses a living artistic idea. Performance, then, is a living artistic idea: *performance is malleable conceptual matrix that creates, holds, develops, and explores an embodied artistic idea and/or expression*.

Patrick Grafton-Cardwell (2020) argues against two types of monism that assess when or how a work of art is complete by claiming the following thesis:

> **Completion Pluralism:** There are many kinds of artwork completion, many corresponding senses of "completion," and no kind of artwork completion is objectively more important than any other. (198)

For Grafton-Cardwell, as well other aestheticians, the premise of their claims and arguments surrounding the completion of art is that *art comes to a completion*. Grafton-Cardwell's general thesis is that the completion of an artwork can be considered complete using many different properties and metrics.

66 BETWEEN THE LINES

I would suggest, however, that the case of (text-based) theatre poses a problem to a basic presumption made by Grafton-Cardwell and the field: conceived as a work of art, there is no real end to the artistic act of a *play*, as a play is never really *complete*, per se. While there is an end to a dramatic text (with the occasional exception of rewrites by the playwright[14]), the dramatic text is just one (albeit major) component of theatre and the artistic life of a play. And while there is an end to a specific performance of a specific play, multiple performances of a play and the play's performance history are also a part of the play as a piece of art.

The Problem Case of Theatre

Before we dive into the world of theatre, let me define a few terms as I am using them here. "Theatre" is an artistic medium that is comprised of dramatic literature and performance(s). A "play" is a specific piece of theatre art. As such, a *play* is comprised of a dramatic text + performance$_1$ + performance$_2$ + performance$_3$ + . . . *ad infinitum*. So plugging in an example, *Hamlet* is a piece of theatre. *Hamlet* is a play that is the combination of William Shakespeare's dramatic text, *Hamlet*, and many performances of *Hamlet*. These terms are important since one of the first seminal debates in aesthetics and theatre studies played out concerning the relationship of a dramatic text to the performance of the dramatic text.

Noël Carroll (2001), David Z. Saltz (2001), and James R. Hamilton (2001) debated whether the performance (of a play) constitutes its own art form or is merely an interpretation of a dramatic text, and therefore is once removed from the original artistic creation. Much later, after (at least) theatre studies widely accepted the idea that performance is its own art form, building off of Hamilton (2001, 2007), and in Bennett (2017), I claimed that there is no possibility of reproducing the dramatic text and that every single production

THE NATURE OF VIEWING THEATRE   67

of a play is, in essence, an *adaptation*, and, thus, an original piece of art.

My 2017 assertion that every performance of a play is an adaption not only addresses the above conversation about the relationship between text and performance, but more relevant here, it gets to the never-ending nature of theatre, as the embodiment of the text has different material realities each time. The embodiment of different characters by different actors' real bodies creates and changes the material reality of the performance among different performances, and this does not even take into account the matter of interpretation. That is, so much of the embodiment of a play happens in the fleshing out of what is not written in the speeches and stage directions, some more intentional than other changes, such as the color palate of the lighting design versus the real bodies of the actors or the shape of the theatre and what type of stage it has. Given this notion of adaption, then, each production is a part of the play (as a whole) but also, in part, is its own piece of art. As such, there is always some new artistic creation (or "re-creation" as I call it) in the life of a play.

Art Objects versus Experiencing Art

Theatre is the most obvious artistic medium, or, at least, the most extreme example, of artwork that is not complete, and that is why I began with it. Theatre makes most obvious the difference between, say, the *existence of an artistic object*, such as a dramatic text, and the experience of *experiencing an artistic object*, such as listening and watching an embodied performance of the text. In general, the former, the artistic object, *may* be complete, but the latter, the experiencing of the artistic object, is just as important to consider in this debate over the completion of a work of art. After all, a novel, say, does not do much as a work of art without being read, or a painting does not do much as a work of art without being

68   BETWEEN THE LINES

seen. That is, the reception of, or experience of receiving the observational data from, the artwork is inherently a part of the art. That is, art does not really *end*. While Jorge Luis Borges, in two of his most famous stories—"The Library of Babel" and "Pierre Menard, the Author of the *Quixote*"—really gets at this subtle distinction in regard to literature, Borges's distinction between *art-as-an-object* versus *art-as-an-experience* speaks, as far as I can tell, to all art forms.

Borges's "The Library of Babel" speaks of a seemingly infinite library that contains practically infinite books that contain every combination of letters and spaces within five hundred pages, thus containing every book ever written or will be written, plus nonsensical books. The issue is that while the narrator suggests the infinite nature of the library, there are, mathematically speaking, a finite number of number and letter combinations within five hundred pages. But the idea that the library is infinite still holds: that is, as people spend their entire life in this library, even if they read the same book again later in life, they will have a different experience of the book and, thus, each book is always new and/or different.

Similarly, in "Pierre Menard, the Author of the *Quixote*," where a twentieth-century writer "writes" (or, rather, copies or simply says he wrote) the entire text of Miguel Cervantes's *Don Quixote*. The idea, wrapped in dry sarcasm, is that the text is always different based upon the context in which it is being read, as reading (or writing) *Don Quixote* in sixteenth-century Spain is vastly different than reading it in either twentieth-century Argentina, or (now) in the twenty-first century (in the English-speaking world). That is, the experience of reading Cervantes's *Don Quixote* is always different, whether it is between vastly different people over vast times and places or within one's own lifetime.

It is due to all of these above factors that viewing performance is, counterintuitively, not a shared experience but a highly subjective individual experience that is modified by the presence of other minds in the public realm. On one hand, theatre incorporates

THE NATURE OF VIEWING THEATRE   69

other minds, views, and opinions in such a way that we are not, as Descartes argued, individual minds (*I think, therefore I am*). Instead, we are social beings whose minds are shaped by other minds. Yet, on the other hand, Wittgenstein's notion that we only understand the world via a shared reality because of language is not right either, as we have vastly different understandings and experiences when viewing performance. Stated again, *viewing performance is a highly individualized experience that, paradoxically, relies on the experiences of other minds.*

While "empathy" may be a shared experience in the theatre and performance—and (via Keith Lehrer) each observer's mirror neurons are observing the same object to *mirror* (though, *if* all facing the same way, of course)—an audience is a random set of eyes, ears, and minds (though, usually from higher-income households with higher education levels). The point is that the facts going into the play—or, rather, the facts *about*, and *circumstances of*, the individual observers and what each observer "attends to" and what/which emotions are brought into the theatre space at any given two-hour or so span of time—are not evenly dispersed among the audience members (and even participants). Some know the play line by line, others know the main stage directions, some have just read it, some have just seen it, and some do not even know the play at all.

Each "spectator," then, uses and/or has a different *lens*, or "spectacle," through which he or she experiences a (largely similarly viewed) object or action. Thus, truth needs to be revealed by the experiences and thoughts of everyone included to have something like Pollock's objective justified belief possible, given that the "spectacles" are going to be slightly different for each "spectator," to play off the title of, and some of the ideas in, Dennis Kennedy's *The Spectator and the Spectacle*. The spectators each spectate through their own unique and subjective circumstances (to think back to our "*evening at the theatre*"), which, rarely, is steady (even for each spectator), as circumstances change based upon new information

70 BETWEEN THE LINES

and experiences. Theatre and performance are always different, inevitably different, even if the words and actions are *exactly* the same (which is essentially impossible), because the audience is *always* a different audience.[15] This is true even when it is just one reader, one actor, or one spectator. It is not only that the physical composition or location generally changes in an audience, but the knowledge both personally experienced and acquired from other minds changes over the course of a day or two, if not decades or centuries. This is the very point made by Heraclitus, in the epigraph to this chapter.

An experience I had in my teens at the theatre may prove useful here. During the drive into New York City to see *Smokey Joe's Cafe* on Broadway, I asked my mom what the musical was about. As I remember hearing it, she told me that it was a "typical musical." Once it started, though, I was having trouble following the characters from scene to scene, and I thought the character development was terrible. During intermission, my mom asked what I thought about it, and I told her that I loved the music but was having trouble following the plot. Her response stuck with me: "What kind of plot would there be in a musical revue?" Once that single word was added, I adored the second half of the musical revue. Hence, that night, I watched two different shows: first, an undeveloped musical and, then, second, a thoroughly entertaining musical revue. However, while the act of triangulating the experiences of spectators gives each a better understanding of the object/performance commonly viewed, this activity poses some further problems. To discuss these ideas with more precision, I need two helpful terms: *qualia* and "propositional attitudes." In short, individual instances of experience are called *qualia* (*quale* is singular); the attitudes/feelings/beliefs one has toward a proposition are called "propositional attitudes." After consulting with another mind during intermission (i.e., my mom), the *qualia* remained intact, in terms of how I experienced the first half of the show; my propositional attitude toward the first half changed to a

THE NATURE OF VIEWING THEATRE 71

degree. However, with the newfound knowledge about the show, my propositional attitude and the *qualia* certainly changed for the second half of the show.

Before the intermission, the *qualia* presented in a way that I felt like I was experiencing a disjointed musical. The propositional attitude was one of "*I dislike that* the musical is disjointed" (for added clarity, here, the *propositional attitude* is italicized; the proposition is underlined). During intermission, after finding out that it is supposed to be a "musical revue," the qualia regarding the first act did not change, per se. However, I understood, now, why my "propositional attitude" changed ("*I, now, understand why I thought that* the musical is disjointed"). Heading into the second half of the show, my individual experience was entirely different. The qualia presented itself as a musical revue, and my "propositional attitude" changed drastically to "*I love that* I am watching this musical revue." In short, my attitude toward the show changed because both the "proposition" and the qualia changed *to me* (even though, in fact, little to nothing about the show itself changed between the first half and the second half). What caused this change was the knowledge I gained from another mind, which *changed the circumstances from which I was experiencing* the performance.

However, further, what has happened to my experiences and attitudes over the years? What has happened to those qualia and propositional attitudes, with my fading memory of that experience and, now, having more knowledge about theatre and performance? Besides a snippet or two of visual memories of the set and actors and auditory memories of the music, all that I remember *now* is the first fifteen minutes of the show, the disjointedness I experienced during those first fifteen minutes, my attitude toward the show, and the *fact* that I remember that my attitude and experience changed after intermission.[16]

In short, an art object may exist, but the experiencing of that art object is not usually time-place-person specific. (The notable exception to this is that some performance art and performance artists

72 BETWEEN THE LINES

cannot replicate the experience of some one-off performances.) The artwork is ongoing since the experience of that art object will be different each time. Sometimes the differences are due to differences in the art object itself (as in the case of theatre, or more subtly, in music or dance). Other times, there are differences in regard to receiving the observational data of the art object (as in the case of literature, painting, sculpture, architecture, etc.). But either way, the experience of an art object is never complete, as it is, or at least can be, always changing. And it is because of this that the experiences and insights of a bevy of participants and observers must be triangulated to approach a truer understanding of a piece of theatre.

4

The Nature of Theatre's Empty Spaces

Thus far, I have been concerned about (1) *what exists* in theatre and (2) *viewing what exists* in the theatre. But, as stated in the Introduction, so much of theatre, conceptually, resides between the lines. Therefore, here, I want to examine the empty spaces of theatre. These empty spaces have many implications for understanding both the ontology of theatre and the epistemology of theatre.

In the most general of senses, the *worlds* of theatre are *utopias* (i.e., "nowhere[s]"). What are these theatrical worlds? Do they exist? Where do they exist? And how are we to understand these so-called worlds? I would answer these questions by suggesting that "theatrical places"—"*theatri topia*"—reside mostly in the spaces between the lines of a dramatic text (in traditional text/script-based theatre). It is in this space of nothing (i.e., between the lines)—or "nowhere"—where much of the theatrical world resides. This is where "nowhere," and *utopia*, can be found: one foot in ordinary language and one foot in imagination. Pure imagination—the language of young children before they are fully shaped and bound by language—*can* imagine a world or a part of a world that simply does not, or even *cannot*, exist. For adults, however, as a reflection of our world, language is meant to make the world appear logical; language works to smooth over the incomplete and the incongruous.

Coherence and Correspondence

The coherence theory of truth and the correspondence theory of truth are both, more or less, historical concepts that emerged

---

Between the Lines. Michael Y. Bennett, Oxford University Press. © Oxford University Press 2024.
DOI: 10.1093/9780197691700.003.0005

74 BETWEEN THE LINES

during the birth of analytic philosophy. Proponents of the coherence theory of truth, such as F. H. Bradley, opine that the truth of a statement or a belief can only be judged in terms of how well it coheres with other held statements or beliefs, and as such, truth is thought of as degrees of truth. However—and relatively speaking, in opposition—the correspondence theory of truth, with proponents such as Bertrand Russell and G. E. Moore, holds that something is true if it corresponds with a fact and/or a state of affairs. Since this book will not attempt to make any inroads into conversations surrounding coherence and/or correspondence theories of truth, I will abstain from going into more detail, as these explanations are sufficient for the purposes of this book.

In terms of our subject, theatre does what VGA computer monitors of the late 1980s attempted to do: make 256 colors feel, or *cohere* in a manner that felt, *as though* we are viewing millions or an infinite number of colors, as a means to smooth over the incomplete. So that the playtext coheres when on the stage, theatre requires extratextual *correspondence* to our world. "Existing" between the lines, these extratextual elements are the blank spaces of theatre that need to be filled in by performance(s). Whether or not a play corresponds to our world or coheres has much to do with what is written, but much, too, has to do with what is not written. In short, in theatre, between the lines is where all of the fun happens.

Subsumption and Distinctness

In between these lines in the theatre, and related to the ideas of coherence and correspondence, it is also clear that while not explicitly stated, there are *other things* that exist, too, either as implied and/or imagined objects. We can chalk this up to the phenomenon of *fictional incompleteness*. That is, fictional incompleteness is the idea that a piece of fiction does not (or even cannot) say everything about its fictional characters and fictional world, as there are limits both with language and time, as well as space concerns. Thus far,

THE NATURE OF THEATRE'S EMPTY SPACES   75

the literature on fictional incompleteness has largely dealt with *truths* that are contained in the fiction that are over and above what a *narrator* says. To deal with truths that are not made explicit by the narrator, philosophers have turned to the "explicit content" (Stokke 2021: 68) found in fiction and the ideas of *importation* (Gendler 2000; Stokke 2021) and, much more often, *generation* (Walton 1990; Davies 1996; Woodward 2011; Friend 2017). Most recently Stokke has tried to demonstrate the differences between generation and importation: generation explains things that are not told by the narrator (Stokke 2021: 67), while importation includes things not made explicit but are based upon what is told by the narrator (Stokke 2021: 67–68). These above concepts help Stokke distinguish between the *fictional record* of a story (which is made up of what is said by the narrator as well as information that is imported) and the *fictional truths* of a story (that which is true in the fictional world) (Stokke 2021: 68). I am engaging with Stokke, not only because the concepts of importation and generation help clarify my argumentation below, but mostly because the literature thus far, including Stokke, has focused almost exclusively on prose fiction (which contains a narrator).

But with theatre, there are *two* different art forms (see, especially, Hamilton 2007): the dramatic text, which we read, and theatrical performance(s), which we watch. When reading the dramatic text, first, there is *no narrator*, though the stage directions can function, at times, something like a narrator setting the stage, and even giving color to the characters and/or set. Therefore, in plays without a narrator (which is the vast, vast majority), Stokke's concept of importation is rendered moot, as extratextual information cannot come from an absent narrator. Second, in theatrical performance, much of the implicit content found in the reading process that can be generated is actually fleshed out in performance, with literal bodies and objects in real space. Thus, while the concepts of importation and generation are useful, they have not yet been adequately applied to theatre. By addressing theatre, specifically, as a unique art form (both in the reading and the watching of a play), I suggest that two concepts from philosophical semantics, *subsumption* and *distinctness*, can be applied, expanded, and slightly modified, to further aid us in this quest to offer a systematic account of theatre. Subsumption refers to the idea that larger, if you will, objects and statements have smaller, if you will, parts subsumed within. Distinctness refers to the idea when objects/statements are unique and do not overlap. Given that dramatic texts only contain a limited amount of information in the form of words and statements that often refer to objects, these two concepts are vital for how plays cohere and/or correspond.

It may be argued that I should merely use the two concepts of importation and generation and simply apply them to the theatre. However, subsumption and distinctness are concepts used by philosophical linguists and, specifically, in *situation semantics*, where linguistic expressions are evaluated in relation to *partial worlds*, serving as an alternative to possible world semantics (Kratzer 2019). Situation semantics presents a *local* approach (e.g., Kratzer and Arregui), whereas traditional accounts of the possible worlds thesis (e.g., Lewis and Stalnaker) take a *global* approach.[1] Given that the dramatic text creates (or "re-creates") a theatrical world, but does so in an incomplete, partial manner, thinking about partial worlds is, in many ways, more analogous to the world of a play, and hence it makes more sense to use the terms "subsumption" and "distinctness" from situation semantics.

To demonstrate the distinct (or *distinctness*) and the subsumed (or *subsumption*), let us start with the idea of *subsumption*, taking the following example about Paula and a lunatic, by Shai Cohen:

> PAULA: Yesterday evening I only painted this still life over there.
> LUNATIC: That's not true. You painted these apples too.
> (Cohen 2009: 1)

As Cohen suggests, "In case these apples are part of this assortment of fruit, the Lunatic's denial of Paula's claim is false. Intuitively,

THE NATURE OF THEATRE'S EMPTY SPACES   77

painting a part of something does not add anything to painting the whole; therefore, the fact that Paula painted these apples does not falsify her claim that she only painted this still life" (2009: 1). That is, the part—that is, the painting of apples—is subsumed within the larger whole—that is, the painting of the still life—where the still life contains the apples. If I suggest that "I have a heap of sand," to play off the sorites paradox, then the idea that I have individual grains of sand in that heap is subsumed by the statement that I have a heap of sand. I would not say, therefore, "I have a heap of sand and I have grains of sand."

Related to the idea of subsumption is the idea of *distinctness*. As explained, again, by Cohen, "Assume that A in fact painted this still life, and that these apples are part of it. In this case, B is justified in denying A's claim. Still, B's sentence with *too* is infelicitous. In some sense, painting something and painting part of it are not *distinct* happenings" (Cohen 2009: 3). Cohen continues:

> Distinctness seems to be essential to counting. Kratzer (2007) observes, following Geach (1980), that if there is a teapot on the table, then there is also a part of that teapot on the table which is itself a teapot, for example the one consisting of all the parts of the bigger teapot minus one millimeter of the spout. Still, we wouldn't say that there are two teapots on the table. There must be some principle to the effect that a counting domain cannot contain overlapping individuals. (Cohen 2009: 3)

Here, Cohen concludes the following, in simple language: "It seems then that two things are distinct if and only if they do not overlap" (2009: 3).[2] In our case of the apples and the still life painting, the apples overlap with the apples in the still life painting. Therefore, the apples are not distinct from the still life painting. Again, the still life painting subsumes the painting of the apples. Going back to the sorites paradox, if I were to have a (single) "heap of sand" that, let us say, made up of 2,647 grains of sand, I would

78 BETWEEN THE LINES

not say that I had 2,647 heaps of sand; nor would I say, I have three heaps of sand (within my single larger heap of sand).

To complicate this line of reasoning, Peter Thomas Geach brings up the problem of whether a teapot would remain a single teapot if a small piece were chipped off—would you now have two teapots or even a multiplicity of teapots within a single teapot (1980: 215)? By using a "teacup," rather than a teapot, what if instead of just chipping off a piece of the teacup, the entire teacup handle cleanly breaks off. I would suggest that we do not have two teacups, now; however, we do—now—have a single *cup* and a single *handle*: two *distinct* parts of the teacup as a whole. This example of a teacup that can be divided into two distinct parts is analogous to properties in the theatre.

Subsumed Properties in the Theatre

It is easy to understand how a grain of sand can be subsumed within a heap of sand or how a painting of an apple is subsumed within a still life painting. A grain of sand or a painted apple are *constituent parts* of, respectively, a heap of sand or a still life painting. However, theatre presents a slightly different model of subsumption than the model established by our still life painting or heap of sand examples. In theatre, with so much of the art form, itself, not specified in the art, I claim that subsumption does not only describe constituent parts of a whole, but that, in theatre, most of the *properties* of a theatrical character (and theatrical world) exist, if you will, via *subsumption*. We can similarly say that the subsumed properties of a theatrical character or a theatrical world are *derived* properties, coming from within the *complex* properties and situations that are specified in the text. That is, to return to Stokke's language, the explicit content of a play, its spoken words/speeches, does not elucidate many properties associated with the characters.

THE NATURE OF THEATRE'S EMPTY SPACES 79

Therefore, the majority of properties of a theatrical character do not come from the importation of information from a narrator, as a narrator does not exist in theatre (with some rare exceptions). Instead, most of the properties of a theatrical character come from within the spoken words/explicit content. The properties of a theatrical character, then, are subsumed *within the explicit content*. That is, the concept of importation does not specify where the extratextual information comes from (or, rather, importation is a broad term that covers the many ways that extratextual information comes into being, whether implicitly, or not even implicitly, from the narrator); whereas subsumption more accurately describes in the theatre where nondistinct properties emerge as subsumption implies that the information is *contained within* the object(s) being examined.

I claim that there are three *types of properties* associated with theatrical characters and worlds: *distinct properties*, *subsumed properties*, and *truthful properties*. The case of theatre presents some special issues for the philosophy of art, as there are some properties—like Hamlet's brilliance, for example—that are (a) widely accepted but (b) perhaps more challenging to see how they might be derived from the explicit. These properties are the subsumed properties that are found within the text that are not explicitly stated as distinct properties. That is, theatrical characters have properties that go beyond what is in the text, and these properties are derived—via entailment, actual generic connections, and/or whole/parts connections—from the text in combination with facts about the actual world. Whether or not we can call these processes importation or generation, in trying to capture the various ways in which further, unstated facts about fictions can be true of them, we can think about what is derived from certain distinct facts as such: A is F can generate further facts, such as A's being G. One way is that being F can *entail* being G; or another way is that it can be a *generic* fact, such as F (humans) are G (have ears).

80 BETWEEN THE LINES

Both entailment and generic facts aid in thinking about distinct and subsumed properties of a theatrical character in theatre. That is, as I have suggested elsewhere, Hamlet is the sum total of everything he says and does in the play (Bennett 2017: 32). As such, we can think of every single thing that Hamlet says and does *as explicit content in the dramatic text*. To demonstrate this, let us think more about the play *Hamlet*. We can say that there is the distinct character, Hamlet, or we can also say that there is the distinct place, Elsinore. Now, we know many distinct facts about Hamlet, for example that he is a prince and that he dies at the end of the play. We also have every reason to believe that Hamlet is human, and presumably, then, humans also have two ears and a nose. However, do we know anything specific about the shape of Hamlet's ears or his nose? No, but the fact that the actor who plays Hamlet ought to have two ears and a nose is subsumed within the fact that he is a human. That is, there are subsumed *generic* properties that are derived other distinct properties (e.g., *having-two-ears* due to *being-human*). Similarly, while we observe "a platform before the castle," we are not told that the nature of the columns or the thickness of the walls that that hold up this "platform," but we do know that such walls or columns exists. These elements, then, such as Hamlet's nose and ears and the walls or columns that hold up the platform before the castle, are *subsumed within the play* and will or can appear on the stage: either they will be present by necessity (as humans have noses and ears, the actor playing Hamlet will also have two ears and a nose), or they can be present (as in whether the walls will be visible that hold up the platform). But to add to the complexity here, Hamlet is, arguably, quite brilliant. But where is this in the play? *Being-brilliant* is never attributed to Hamlet in the play. Since nothing explicitly ties Hamlet with the property of *being-brilliant*, we must suggest that the brilliance within the distinct and stated properties attributed to Hamlet is *entailed* within what he says and does (i.e., *being-brilliant* is subsumed within what Hamlet says and does).

The Role of the Actor/Director in Theatrical Coherence and Subsumption

Much of the truth of the play comes through the actors on stage. The actor must consider distinct facts—or rather, distinct events and/or things—and figure out what is subsumed within. The director must weigh those distinct events against the desire to form a cohesive narrative: the idea that theatrical characters are participants in the world of the play "suggests not a linear externally-imposed narrative that each character fits into in their own role in the narrative, but a collection of internally-derived ensemble personal narratives, the latter being how real life operates."[3] The task for the directors and actors is to take these distinct facts, made most obvious, for example, in a history play, and figure out what is subsumed within. This is how theatre coheres.

Thinking about a character's distinct properties and their subsumed properties in the dramatic text, then, offers the director and actor an entirely new way to cast and embody a character, without thinking as much about necessary strict adhesion to a dramatic text. That is not to say, anything goes (or *should* go) in theatre and is allowable and/or is truthful to the dramatic text, but that thinking about distinctness and subsumption help thread the needle between something that is necessarily *true* versus something *truthful*, if you will, which mimics the difference between a fictional character being true versus a fictional character embodying something truthful. In Oscar Wilde's play *The Importance of Being Earnest* (1895), for example (and this will be discussed in detail later in this book), it is *not true* that Lady Bracknell has a male body, but when played by a male actor, this embodiment says something *truthful* about Lady Bracknell.

In Sum

This book has made, and will continue in Part II to make, a number of related assertions about (a) theatre as an art form; (b) properties

82 BETWEEN THE LINES

associated with theatrical characters and theatrical worlds; and (c) the difference between something *being true* in theatre versus something *being truthful* in the theatre. First, I claim that there are three types of properties associated with theatrical characters and theatrical worlds: distinct properties, subsumed properties, and truthful properties:

1. *Distinct properties* are found explicitly in the dramatic text and are necessarily *true* (e.g., Hamlet is the Prince of Denmark).
2. *Subsumed properties* are derived from the distinct properties that are explicit in the dramatic text, and these properties, which can be true, are derived either
   a. by *entailment* (e.g., Hamlet is human),
   b. by entailment in combination with other *generic facts* (e.g., Hamlet has two ears and a nose), or
   c. by *interpretation* (and/or *triangulation*) of available distinct facts (e.g., Hamlet is brilliant).
3. *Truthful properties* are a type of subsumed properties that may or may not be *truly* applied to a character (i.e., they may even be *falsely* applied to a character) and also may not be derived from any of the above ways, but yet these subsumed properties speak to something *truthful* about theatrical characters and/or theatrical worlds (e.g., Lady Bracknell can best be understood as a "domineering," *Alpha male*, and played by a male actor conveys this better than if played by a female actor). A truthful property contains at least one truth, even if the overall state of that object is false. These properties may be thought of as *truthful suggestions* and are derived
   a. by relations in the text that are weaker than entailment, namely *textual assertions that do not necessarily fit the actual world* (e.g., The Ghost of King Hamlet should be about the same height as a human), or
   b. by *truthful suggestions* that are not implied by any of the above ways but simply *make sense*, if you will, or *can*

THE NATURE OF THEATRE'S EMPTY SPACES   83

make sense (e.g., Richard III must have been bullied in his childhood).

Second, there are two processes/types of objects that exemplify these three properties that come into being by one or both of two ways in the theatre: "re-creation" and/or the "re-positioning" of objects/"re-positioned" objects:

1. *Re-creation* describes both the process and the abstract object that comes into being through a recombination and/or unique cluster of actually existing, concrete and/or abstract objects, where we can call the resultant object *a re-created object*.
2. *Re-positioning* describes the process by which actually existing objects are viewed/presented in a manner that explores novel relations among its constituent parts. The resultant object that is viewed/presented is a *re-positioned object*.

Both of these processes and the objects that come into being through these processes are expressed through one or more of the three following figurative expressions: (1) metaphor, (2) representation, and/or (3) presentation.

Through its investigation of these figurative expressions, *Between the Lines: A Philosophy of Theatre* posits that theatre and performance serve the supremely important function, both individually and societally, of testing out unknown situations, by investigating what might, what could, and what could not be the case. By setting up the (fictional/fictionalized) characters and contexts that are contrary to the facts of the world (i.e., the counterfactual antecedent), the playwright allows us to see this (unknown) situation play out according to (known) human nature. Because the conceptual spaces between the lines highlight the *variables* found in theatre, theatrical performance allows us to test out not only what is possible but also what is *true* in *our* world.

84 BETWEEN THE LINES

This book examines the *input* of performance and, more specifically, the conceptual spaces of performance: not only what is implied or tenuously exists (such as offstage characters or offstage actions or offstage subplots and context) but the empty spaces of the dramatic text (and some performance) that give rise to performance's variability. In other words, instead of thinking solely about what is written, I also want to look at *what is not written*, and what the unwritten does for/to performance. That is, the dramatic text, while admittingly also giving guidance and direction for the production in the form of stage directions, exists mostly as the auditory part of performance, from whence only one part of the intellectual thrust of a theatrical performance derives. Ultimately, however, it is in the search and understanding of these metaphorical blank spaces that theatre breeds and encourages curious behaviors, which serve individual and societal growth and are much needed in this so-called post-truth world.

PART II
SPACES OF THEATRE

*Offstage Characters, Imagined Objects, and Other
Prickly Philosophical Problems in Theatre*

PART II

5

Distinctness in Theatre

Theatrical Language and Events

Given that much of performance and most of the reading experience come from theatrical speeches, and that other properties in a play derive from the distinct facts that are stated in these theatrical speeches, the following two questions need to be posed: (1) What is theatrical language? and (2) Does, and/or how does, theatrical language differ from everyday speech?

In the most basic and obvious sense, some words function as *subjects*, some as *predicates*, other words function as *prepositions*, as *modals*, and others as *indexicals*. J. L. Austin's "performatives"—for example, "*I now pronounce you man and wife*" and "*I name this ship 'The Queen Mary'*"—were revolutionary because the propositions in these statements offered an alternative to the dichotomous truth value of a statement that preoccupied the logical positivists, as these propositions are neither "true" nor "false," but perform a function of some sort. That is, the above-mentioned performatives, respectively, consecrate a marriage and name a ship, versus being true or false. Up until that point when Austin came up with performatives, philosophers and linguists were concerned with whether the propositional content of a statement was true or false. So Austin changed the conversation with his performatives.

I only open with Austin's now-defunct notion of "performatives" (as it was, in fact, Austin who realized their limitations and came up with, instead, the concepts of locutionary, illocutionary, and perlocutionary acts), not because I want to engage with Austin's performatives, but because Austin used "performatives" to

Between the Lines. Michael Y. Bennett, Oxford University Press. © Oxford University Press 2024.
DOI: 10.1093/9780197691700.003.0006

88 BETWEEN THE LINES

demonstrate a special case of language usage that, at the time, had not yet been considered and/or elucidated. I am only interested in Austin to analogously note that there is *another* specific situation where the utterance of propositions has a function that has similarly not yet been elucidated.

In short, some theatrical utterances constitute a special case of language usage: I claim that utterances of statements with propositional content in theatre function as *events*. Many theatrical utterances do not *correspond* to our world. Instead, the role of language in the theatre is to create an *internally coherent* world of the play, of which *that* world *corresponds to a truth in our world*, or that world *portrays something truthful about our world*. And the event is the portrayal of something true and/or truthful.

Speech Act Theory and Events

There is a vast field of study about *events*, but almost without exception, the focus of philosophers and linguists (and all in between or beyond) is on defining what *is* an event or how to *refer* to an event.[1] That is, the two main questions pondered are these: (1) How do we describe the ontology of an event? and/or (2) How do we describe and/or understand the language about, or referring to, an event? These two questions are asked about events that broadly fall into the realm of *actions* or *states*. But what if the utterance of a statement containing a proposition is an event itself? Theatrical language is a special case of language usage that offers the philosopher, linguist, and literary/arts critic (all broadly defined) a different angle to consider thinking about both what an event is and how to describe an event.

However, even more basic to playtexts and the logic of theatre, there exists a presumption, regardless of the naturalness or experimental nature of the language within a play, that the language

DISTINCTNESS IN THEATRE   89

within a play operates in the same manner that it does in *our* world. This is not the case, though, in theatre.

The two closest corollaries to the language in theatre are (1) *metaphor* and (2) *sarcasm*. Both metaphor (and allegory, too) and sarcasm discuss one thing, yet mean/intend something else. Theatrical language, too, has this same function and works on two levels as well. But, by and large, theatrical speeches (and their propositional contents) in playtexts are not written or uttered metaphors, nor are they are saying the exact opposite of what is said (as in sarcasm). Instead, unlike sarcasm, where the opposite of what is uttered is meant, and also unlike in metaphor, which similarly works on two levels—one the literal understanding of the utterance and one the figurative interpretation of the utterance— the utterance of propositional content in theatre is tripartite: (1) an utterance in theatre is a subject/predicate of an unpronounced *indexical pointing to a specific state of affairs*; (2) performs a *function* in that the counterfactual condition is projected forward in the type of response/action; and (3) is a part, functions as, or *is the event* itself that the audience is there to witness. There is a fourth element, too: *metaphorical interpretation* is the outgrowth of this tripartite structure.

The *artifice of theatre* is that the propositional content contained in the playtext functions as an extended indexical that directs us/ situates us/points to an extended counterfactual condition, which is the fictional world of the play. The *reality of theatre*, however, is that the utterances of the propositional content in statements contained in the playtext function as and *are the event* of theatre. That is, the words and statements that create and constitute the propositional content of theatrical utterances within theatre function as subjects, predicates, modals, and so on *within* the fictional world of the play. However, *outside* of the world of the play—to the audience—*the utterances of the propositions contained in theatrical statements function as, and are, the theatrical event* itself.

90 BETWEEN THE LINES

"Strike Three. You're Out!"

Before I get to language in theatre, I first want to take you out to a ballgame. Language in baseball provides a good example to build a transitory bridge to the language in the theatre. Referees at professional sporting events, especially obvious in the case of umpires in baseball, use language that has three functions (of course, used in the context of a baseball game and spoken by the umpires). "Ball," "Strike," "Safe," and "Out" (1) function as in ordinary language as predicates of an unpronounced indexical; (2) are utterances that perform a function in the game; and (3) furthermore, function as (a part of) the *event*.

For example, first, when the Homeplate Umpire at a baseball game calls "Ball," "Ball" functions as a predicate of an unpronounced indexical which (though unstated) points to a specific state of affairs (i.e., "This is a ball." That is, the ball that was thrown by the pitcher did not pass over homeplate and/or through the strike zone). Second, the utterance of "Ball" is not only a predicate (or even functions in some way as an indexical) that attempts to describe a specific state of affairs (possesses a sense of indexicality), but the call of "Ball" performs a function in the game, affecting the future performance and playing out of the game. However, furthermore, the refereeing of a sporting event is a part of, functions as, and *is* the sporting *event* itself as well.

Theatre: Moveable Referents

Elsewhere, I discuss theatrical language and interpretation, suggesting that there is a "moveable limit" in interpretation between dramatic text and theatrical performance:

> a dramatic text [. . .] essentially constitutes a *moveable limit* because since a dramatic text is a somewhat-incomplete artistic

DISTINCTNESS IN THEATRE 91

expression because, as I suggest in the relatively simple statement, in the theatre (in general),

> (Character) A intends (Character) B to understand p, but the audience—through the utterance of p—who also understands p, understands an open-ended q, as well.

Interpretation, then—even if it were possible to experience the exact same reality—will be wildly varied, and, thus, while the words do not change (though, sometimes plays are later edited), the contexts and readers of those words do, and thus, there is an inherent stability with the utterances of p, but there is instability in the referents associated with q.[2]

Using this above notion of theatrical language, in William Shakespeare's *Hamlet*, the focus is not on the play within the play— that is, the focus is not on *The Murder of Gonzago* within *Hamlet*— that is, not on the p in the play within the play, but the focus is on the q derived from *The Murder of Gonzago*, or the q the way that Claudius interprets it. Hamlet's purpose of The Mousetrap—of the players staging *The Murder of Gonzago*—was in no way to have the audience, and most particularly Claudius, hear and take in the p (i.e., *The Murder of Gonzago*). Hamlet's sole intention was for Claudius to take away the q (i.e., how Claudius both interprets and reacts to *The Murder of Gonzago*). This is the case for the audience of the play, *Hamlet*, as well.

K. Bach claims that a speech act comprises a multiplicity of actions, each corresponding to a different one within a set of intentions. When words are used on stage (e.g., when an actor is using them as part of his or her performance in *Hamlet*), they should be related to a higher-level speech act. In fiction, as D. Wilson says:

> an author may be simultaneously performing acts of communication on two different levels: a lower-level act of describing a fictional world, and a higher-level act of showing this world to the reader as an example of what is possible, or conceivable.[3]

92 BETWEEN THE LINES

We can, then, say that the utterance of the propositional content of the play within the play is a low-level speech act in that it describes the fictional world of *The Murder of Gonzago*, which yields a high-level speech act wherein Claudius understands that the play is analogous to his own situation and that Hamlet is in the know. However, while p (i.e., the low-level speech act of describing a fictional state of affairs) is stable and q (i.e., the high-level speech act of interpretation) is moveable, the audience does not need to understand q for this to be an event. That is, while the audience of Hamlet is focused on Claudius's understanding of the high-level speech act, the other spectators (i.e., the other characters) in the world of *Hamlet* are witnessing *The Murder of Gonzago*, but these other characters on stage (in *Hamlet*) are not privy to the same information that Claudius (and Hamlet and Horatio) possesses.

M. Brand argues that *events* are spatiotemporal particulars.[4] Thinking about the two plays, *Hamlet* and *The Murder of Gonzago* (the latter, the play within *Hamlet*), the utterance of p_1—for example, Marcellus saying "Something is rotten in the state of Denmark" to Horatio (*Hamlet* 1.4)—does not convey the same propositional content, the same p_1, to the receiver of those utterances (i.e., Horatio) as to the audience members watching Hamlet. That is, the proposition that there is something rotten in Denmark, *now* (as in, in the fictional time and world of the play), is what is being communicated to Horatio. But the "now" is all important, as "Something is rotten in the state of Denmark" is a proposition stated in the present (i.e., using the present participle), but in the context of the rest of the propositions in *Hamlet*, the ps (e.g., $p_2, p_3, p_4, p_5 \ldots$) in the play, and in the context of the gathering of an audience at a particular time and a particular place, the audience understands an open-ended q_1.

Though, of course, presumably, there *is* "something" "rotten" in Denmark at this present moment of this essay's writing and the readers' reading (as, presumably, there does exist a rotting apple

DISTINCTNESS IN THEATRE 93

in a garbage can somewhere in Copenhagen, but that is not *necessarily true*). However, in the case of the utterance of p_1 in the *particular* spatiotemporal situation (i.e., the speaker, the actor playing Marcellus saying p_1 to the receiver, the actor playing Horatio, in front of an audience), the audience understands q_1, where q_1 is that there is something unethical transpiring in the Danish court in the world of the play, or in the fictional world of *Hamlet*. The utterance of p_1 is an integral part of the theatrical event. However, the propositional content of p_1 can either be *false* or *contingently true* outside of the world of the play (even as used in the above *metaphorical* sense, as Denmark is not known to be a corrupt and unethical nation *now*). In short, the propositional content of a *particular* theatrical statement, for example, $p_1, p_2, p_3 \ldots$, whether or not it is true, is only understood, and understood to be true, if p_1 is uttered in a particular time, place, and situation (i.e., during a theatrical event).

If the point of a play is for an audience to understand the propositional contents of a moveable, instable q, within a spatiotemporal particular (the event of the theatrical performance), p_1 (or p_2 or $p_3 \ldots$) is not only an integral part of the spatiotemporal particular which will not stand on its own (as these propositions can be either *false* or *contingently true*), but p_1, furthermore, though apparently universal as the utterance of p, will take place in every faithful performance of Shakespeare's *Hamlet* for eternity. However, because of the *particular* nature of afternoon or nightly performances (i.e., the performance of William Shakespeare's *Hamlet* on a given afternoon or night by a given group of actors in front of a given group of audience members), the propositional content of p (i.e., the propositional content of the play, *Hamlet*) and the propositional content of all of the utterances of statements within *Hamlet* (i.e., all of the statements in the play with propositional content [i.e., $p_1, p_2, p_3, \ldots$]) will forever remain unstable because of the changes among the composition of actors and audience members and differences across different locations and eras.

94 BETWEEN THE LINES

Revelatory Speech and Theatrical Statements: Subsumed Knowledge

In a personal exchange with Susan L. Feagin regarding language in the theatre, Feagin describes the revelatory nature of theatrical speeches:

> we expect the characters' speeches to reveal something— otherwise, what is the point of having them say what they say? But what they reveal might be about themselves deliberately, about themselves unwittingly, about the world, about other characters (again, deliberately or unwittingly), and so on. (For example, when a character lies, and we know they are lying, they may reveal something about themselves rather than about the world. For another example, a character might describe something about the world, and unwittingly reveal something about another character who described the world very differently.)[5]

Here, Feagin makes a simple, but profound point: the reader/audience only gets its information about the story from the characters' speeches, or stated another way, the play is revealed through what the characters say (though, of course, there is the unspoken language of gestures and actions, too). This gets us back to the heart of this book: the entire world of the play, both in reading and performance, is *subsumed* within those speeches (and, by extension, the communication of gestures/actions).

In a novel, say, there is a narrator (whether or not they can be trusted) that reveals the knowledge of the story and the world of the story. However, absent of this in theatre, where are the properties of a character or theatrical world revealed? That is, following Feagin's above observations, each theatrical character is tasked by the playwright to *be* the character and to *say something about* the character (and/or other characters). Therefore, while Bertolt Brecht was outward and dogmatically transparent in his quest to have his actors

DISTINCTNESS IN THEATRE   95

comment upon their own characters in order to alienate the audience to force them to think about versus feel for the character, the (generic) playwright, too, must have (to a lesser degree than Brecht, but still to a degree) characters who are self-revelatory in addition to simply being themselves. This, simply, is theatrical exposition (i.e., contextualizing the world of the play) mixed with theatrical action (i.e., both concrete actions and gestures along with theatrical speeches).

Importantly, knowledge about the play and its characters unfolds for the reader/audience throughout the time of the reading/performance of the play. In "bad" plays, say, we are often aware of the fact that we are learning something about the world of the play or are being given needed knowledge to understand this theatrical world (i.e., the exposition of the play is too obvious):

A BAD PLAY

CHARLOTTE: Oh, hello Mr. Van Dimple, son of a wealthy potato
    farmer, husband to Mrs. Van Dimple, our tragic heroine, and
    father to Anthony Van Dimple, our villain and cause of the
    Van Dimples' consternation.
MR. VAN DIMPLE: Oh, hello, Charlotte, my doting assistant who
    provides me with some needed comic relief.
CHARLOTTE: What is going on with you today?
MR. VAN DIMPLE: In my current state of distress, my son, Anthony,
    has had it out for his mother, and is plotting a no-good plot to
    swindle us for all we are worth. Anthony is a prodigal son . . .

Of course, there are extremes the other way, too: absurd theatre was innovative in the ways in which knowledge and learning were never possible to grasp, either because of utter lack of revelations or because of contradictory revelations (e.g., think of a play by Beckett for the former and a play by Pinter for the latter).

The unfolding, or the revelation, of knowledge is where the enjoyment of theatre resides. However, and here is a key point, the knowledge that one gains is not just knowledge about the plot or knowledge about the characters. That might be the knowledge one is looking for and gaining the first time one encounters a play, whether reading it or seeing it in performance. The dynamism of theatre is that one can see the same play over the years and will not only have different experiences given the different choices made by different directors and actors and designers, but will also be looking for different bits of information that make each viewing experience unique.

Theatrical Tense(s)

In thinking about how we are making bets about future unknown actions in the theatre, the study of theatrical language presents some interesting ways to contemplate the tense of theatre. In its search for truth, whether a play is mimetic or nonmimetic,[6] one peculiarity of theatre is that, for its fictive element to exist in performance, theatre needs to manifest itself through both the very real actor and very real space, and thus (fictional) theatre is bound by the (real) world; the other peculiarity is that theatre happens, it is said, live, in the here and now.

But, of course, while we do not directly observe our world, per se, we watch, read, and study theatre to understand our world. The audience does not go to the theatre to see "lived life," but to watch, I suggest, a "re-creation" of our world (or range of worlds)—where things may be true (i.e., contingent truths are truths that may be true, where they are true in one or more "possible worlds," but not in another/others), but are not necessarily true (i.e., has to be true). A playwright, then, explores truth conditions for one "possible world." In this sense, *a play is an extended counterfactual condition*: *if* [character(s)] *were* [in situation x], *then* . . .

The playwright's formula for writing a play as an extended counterfactual conditional could be slightly different from the above generic formula (i.e., *if* [character(s)] *were* [in situation x], *then*...) should William Archer's notions for playwriting be used. As Archer discusses in his classic 1912 book, *Play-Making*, the germ of a play for a playwright starts from either (1) character or (2) plot. Thus, some possible variants to theatre as an extended counterfactual condition are, *If* [character(s)] *were* [to exist], *then* it would be the case that [the plot/situation] [would proceed in such and such a way]; or *If* [the plot/situation] *were* [to exist/proceed], *then* it would be the case that [such and such (a) character(s)] [would exist]. Obviously, though, the writing of a play is not limited to one of these two formulas for starting a play as outlined in Archer's book.

Let us take a familiar example to demonstrate a play as an extended counterfactual conditional: *if* the uncle of a prince killed the king and married the queen, *then it would be the case* that the prince would seek revenge and die. If these first conditions *were* true (note the *subjunctive*), to be *necessarily true*, it would have to be the case in every "possible world," or in every variation that could take place in our world. This example (i.e., of Hamlet) would demonstrate that given the situation, if the statement were *necessarily true*, then the result would be a logical necessity. However, of course, given that there are other possible scenarios/results in a "possible world" proceeding from this initial situation, this statement is only *possibly/contingently true*.

The notion that theatre is "live" and/or happening in the "present" is firmly planted in our consciousness. However, I think that previous scholarly essays and books in the "liveness"/presentness debate make an uninvestigated presumption that *theatre* is, in fact, "live," "in the present," or "in the here and now." The debate takes the notion of theatrical "liveness" as a simple given, missing the complexity of the liveness that is present (and not present) in theatre. The notion of liveness is a simple approximation of what is happening in theatre, but as I argue, it is (for the most part) not accurate to say that theatre is "live."

98   BETWEEN THE LINES

I contend that the liveness debate has missed and/or overlooked the opportunity to investigate (the presumption/given of) liveness because theatre is generally thought, I argue incorrectly, to be relayed in the present. Common assumptions about theatre suggest that both the dramatic and theatrical narrative generally are happening/told in the present. Consequently, theatre is thought to move toward a future. The tense of theatre, subsequently, is commonly thought to be in the present tense. In this chapter, since Irit Dagani-Raz has argued that theatre can be thought of as an extended *counterfactual condition* (i.e., *if* [it] *were* ___, *then* [it] *would be* ___), my assertion that *the tense of traditional theatre is the past subjunctive* is a straightforward extension of Dagani-Raz's observation. In relation to the debates around liveness/presentness, this critical move (i.e., thinking about theatre in the tense of the past subjunctive) shifts the debate surrounding theatrical liveness from questions of technology and issues of reproducibility to questions of dramatic and theatrical temporality through philosophical and linguistic lenses.[7]

More significantly, this observation that theatre is in the tense of the past subjunctive provides not only an accurate description of the temporality of theatre both in the dramatic text and in performance but provides a key insight into how and why theatre *feels* "live." I suggest that despite/due to the play being in the tense of the past subjunctive—in both in the writing of the traditional playtexts and in the acting process—for theatre to feel "live," each moment of a play must preserve the feeling that all future possibilities are still open. As a counterfactual/subjunctive conditional, drama/theatre relays the feeling of the present by way of enacting the projections that stem from the conditions and variables set in a play's exposition. The exposition in the play creates the presuppositions in the antecedent of a counterfactual condition (i.e., *if* it *were* the case that [these characters were in this situation]). The rest of the play is the projection of these presuppositions (i.e., *then* it *would be* the case that [this is what unfolds]). Explaining the tense and the above

DISTINCTNESS IN THEATRE   99

construction in relation to theatre demonstrates how the playwright and actors (and directors, and entire cast and crew) are able relay the feeling that many possibilities are open at any given moment, imparting the feeling of "liveness."

After introducing the main threads in the conversation that has taken place surrounding liveness, I first examine how the dramatic text relays the feeling that many possibilities are open at any given moment. I suggest that the narrative arc of traditional post-Renaissance drama works on the principle of *possibility*. Second, I discuss how the counterfactual is understood in the text and what the actor, then, can/may/must do to modify the counterfactual statement to impart a feeling of "liveness" in performance. That is, the past subjunctive tense in the text is presupposed as a *two-past mismatched counterfactual*; an actor (and director, etc.) reformulates the presupposition of two-past mismatched counterfactual into the combined presupposition of a *one-past counterfactual* and a "might" counterfactual. These two sections provide the how and why (i.e., the theoretical, linguistic, and philosophical underpinnings) behind theatre's ability to impart the feeling of "liveness" and/or impart the feeling of being in the here and, more particular to this chapter, the now. In short, to present the feeling of liveness—where all possibilities seem as though they are open—in every moment of theatre, the playwright in the text and the entire cast and crew in performance need to create a way to forget the fixed nature of the action.

"Liveness," Thus Far . . .

The idea that theatre happens in the here and now is at the root of Peggy Phelan's well-known arguments about liveness being of central importance to theatre, the impossibility of capturing the performance via technology/media, and the value of experiencing theatre that leaves no trace, witnessed by a limited audience.[8] However,

100   BETWEEN THE LINES

thinking about the requirement for theatre to be "live" is problematic as Philip Auslander discusses in his important book, *Liveness*. Particularly given the current cultural economy where television is the dominant "mediatized" form, Auslander argues that since the rise of television, theatre has become more like television. Thus, Auslander concludes there has been a major easing in the (then-) dividing line between "mediatized" performance and "live" (theatre) performance. The notion of whether "liveness" is something unique, necessary, and/or central to the theatre (and is explored in much more detail and complexity than the above simple summary provides) is a very worthwhile debate. Liveness—or the supposition of witnessing a live story and/or event unfold before your eyes—is *the* (or, at least, *a*) defining feature of theatre versus other types of literature. But this is not the concern of the present book.

Starting from the debate set forth above represented by Phelan and Auslander, Erika Fischer-Lichte usefully describes liveness in terms of "the present"[9]:

> [The topos of presentness] primarily signifies that theatre—unlike epos, novel, or a series of images—does not tell a story taking place at another time and place but portrays events that occur and are perceived by the audience *hic et nunc*. What the spectators see and hear in performance is always present. Performance is experienced as the completion, presentation, and passage of the present.[10]

For Fischer-Lichte, the idea of presentness and the present displayed in liveness is not only a question of a state of being but also a mark of theatre's temporality. The "*hic et nunc*" (i.e., the here and now) is one of the features of theatre, according to Fischer-Lichte, that is created by the "bodily co-presence of actors and spectators."[11] Without directly engaging in the same debate as Fischer-Lichte, this chapter does focus on "the present" that is described by Fischer-Lichte and whether "the present" is integral to "liveness." However,

DISTINCTNESS IN THEATRE 101

it does so by investigating the tense of theatre implied if theatre is conceived as a counterfactual: that the tense of theatre is the past subjunctive.

In short, and for utter clarity, the tense of a counterfactual conditional statement (i.e., *if it were* [the case that], *then it would be* [the case that]) is the past subjunctive. Thus, as parenthetically noted in the above quote from Lewis, counterfactual conditionals are, appropriately so, also called "subjunctive conditionals." Irit Degani-Raz's assertion that theatre is a counterfactual conditional statement, then, allows me take the simple step to assert that the tense (and time) of theatre is in the past subjunctive. This distinction provides the basis for an accurate description of what is, and what is not, "live" in theatre.

Liveness and the Dramatic Arc

The narrative arc of (post-Renaissance) traditional theatre displays abductive logic (and here I am summoning that notion of traditional [mimetic] "theatre" that exists as a useful, but nonexistent category). *Deduction*—which is incorrectly ascribed to the, rather, abductive logic of Sherlock Holmes—requires logical *necessity*: that is, if/given A, then B [*necessarily* follows]. *Abduction*, however, requires a mental leap that defies the rules of logical necessity. Abductive logic—generally conceived as providing the best possible explanation—falls in the realm of logical *possibility*. As I suggest, possibility is needed to maintain the illusion of "liveness." A theatrical character is (usually) defined early in the play, largely through the admixture of exposition and interaction with other characters. For the audience, this process of character definition fixes a set of assumptions about the character and creates reasonable expectations about how the character will act as the play moves on. But this fixing of a set of assumptions about the character, as I am referring to it, does not fix the rules of how the character will act. There is no

102 BETWEEN THE LINES

necessary action (in most traditional post-Renaissance drama) that proceeds from the fixed assumptions about a character.

Greek and Roman tragedies are basically inductive-deductive endeavors where an initial action more or less predetermines the subsequent action, especially with the overarching notion of Fate. Traditional (post-Renaissance) drama, especially starting with Henrik Ibsen, does not usually work on the inductive-deductive spectrum. Traditional (post-Renaissance) drama does equally fix a set of assumptions about characters, but their resultant actions are governed by, and understood by the audience through, probability and possibility.

Narrating and Acting in the Past Subjunctive

A. A. Rini and M. J. Cresswell discuss the perceived overlap between linguistic tense and modal metaphysics in their book, *The World-Time Parallel* (2012). Rini and Cresswell argue that "Times explain tense, not modality . . . At any given moment many possibilities are open to us. As the moment passes, one of these becomes actual."[12] This idea is central to the enactment of theatre because once it has been written, the play has already unfolded. The events of the play are in the past, then, in the sense of past subjunctive. But each moment of theatre through time must suggest that "many possibilities are open to us," or else the performance does not feel "live." How, then, does theatre "live"?

Theatre must be told (both with words and gestures in space) precisely because a play is neither real life nor improvisation.[13] Theatre (in general) has no single narrator, though. And while narrators (i.e., the classic omniscient ones) know the end of the story, the story (even when in the past) does move in a future direction (usually): it unfolds through time. Thus, an actor *narrates* his or her character. "Quoting," rather, is a technique used in narration, but a "quote" is something clearly said in the past. Thus, if

DISTINCTNESS IN THEATRE 103

an actor actually "quoted" his or her character, there is a sense that the story has already played out and future possibilities are already determined.

Given the play is written and, therefore, these future possibilities *are* already closed off, the actor must narrate the past in the present, lest the performance will not feel "live." In this sense, theatre is a fictional past event narrated as if it is an actual event unfolding in the present toward a future where all possibilities are still open. This is only achievable, however, because theatre is narrated in the past subjunctive, which (in essence) sets certain fictional conditions and variables in the past and lets the events unfold. Even though the unfolding is already completed in the past subjunctive, the act of the unfolding, at any given moment within the counterfactual action/utterance, imparts the feeling of the present because "up to that time" when the utterance/action is fully complete, the past events have not yet been actualized. Therefore, the audience feels the openness of future possibilities. That is, the past is actualized; the present is in the moment of actualizing; and the future is what will actualize.

It is precisely because theatre is a counterfactual (and, thus, fictional) that a completed action can appear to be in the present. If theatre were not narrated as a counterfactual, then it would be either a reenactment of history (as something actualized in the past is historical) or an improvisation (without knowing the future arc): history actualized; life is improvised; theatre actualizes counterfactuals. Even when previously rehearsed, during the time of a play, an actor goes through the process (in the present) of actualizing the counterfactual. The "liveness" the audience experiences is the present process of the actor simultaneously remembering and forgetting the narration of his or her character.

What is live in front of the audience, then, is not the plot of a play or the unfolding of a live story, but as I have argued elsewhere, it is necessary for an actor to simultaneously remember and forget how a play plays out.[14] Thus, the liveness we seem to witness on stage is the actor's present act of remembering a past that was necessary

104 BETWEEN THE LINES

to forget. The character is not alive or living in front of us or being observed live by the audience. Rather, it is the acting process of remembering and forgetting that is live. In theatrical performance, then, the story is in the past, and it is the acting process that is in the present: the kicker is that a good actor makes us believe the exact opposite. And the "liveness" that we witness in the theatre is exactly why a "possible world" is stated in the past subjunctive, with its specific subjunctive formulation (i.e., if it *were* ... , *then* ...): theatre works as a past subjunctive that refers, counterfactually, to the present. In a sense, the actor refers to the present in the narrating of a past: but a past that still presents the sense of *future* possibility.

Carlota S. Smith claims that there are three "times" or "temporal perspectives"—Reference Time (following Reichenbach in 1947), Speech Time, and Situation Time—that explain tense:

> Speech Time (SpT) is the center of the system and is the basic default orientation point for temporal expressions. Reference Time (RT) represents the temporal perspective of a sentence; it is simultaneous with, before, or after Orientation Time, which is SpT unless otherwise noted. Situation Time (SitT) is the time of occurrence of a situation: it is simultaneous with, before, or after RT.[15]

In short, natural language, as Smith argues, gives the receiver of an utterance three points of temporal perspective that are used/needed to interpret a statement.

Besides stage directions, there are only speaker headings and speeches in a play. Because the actor has to remember to forget that he or she (and/or some other actor) has uttered these words before, the Speech Time is delivered as though it is in the present. The relations of Reference Time and Situation Time in a play also reify the notion to the audience that something is transpiring now because all of our points of temporal perspective (i.e., Speech Time, Reference Time, and Situation Time) are pointing to the "now." However—and here is the main point of "liveness"—there is an

DISTINCTNESS IN THEATRE 105

unstated presupposition that starts every speech and/or act in theatre: *If character Y were to have said/did what character Y just said/did, then character X would respond by saying/doing,* "_____." This is the basic *modus operandi* of the theatre. And it is precisely because this is left unstated that theatre imparts a feeling as though "many possibilities are open" and, hence, why theatre feels "live."

This idea of the "liveness" of theatre is also set up (from the logic of a linguistic perspective) in terms of the conditions set forth at the beginning of a play. Michela Ippolito argues that "presuppositions in the antecedent of a subjunctive conditional always project."[16] A play's exposition outlines the conditions and variables that essentially make up the *presupposition(s)* of the *antecedent(s)* of a counterfactual. The events that unfold after a play's exposition are the *projections* of the counterfactual. For example, (1) outlines the antecedent of *Hamlet*; (2) outlines the projection of the presuppositions in the antecedent:

(1) *If* it *were* the case that a brilliant young prince *had been away* at college and were to return home after hearing of his father's death, only to find that his mother and uncle have wed, hearing rumors that his uncle (who is now the King) murdered his father, (2) *then* it *would be* the case that this brilliant young prince *would have hatched* a plot to revenge his father's murder.

The antecedent creates a "possible world," and when filled in with other (though not complete) details, becomes—or, rather, *projects*—the presuppositions in the antecedent in the world of the play. Ippolito calls a counterfactual that is set up like this a "*mismatched two-past counterfactual*," describing this type of counterfactual as " 'mismatched' because the past perfect cooccurs with a future adverb."[17] Thus, while there is some confusion in regard to the temporal location and reference of a mismatched two-past counterfactual, the one thing that is certain, however, is that a mismatched two-past counterfactual—which is the basis for

106   BETWEEN THE LINES

theatre—does not describe action taking place in the present. As the projections are already determined, while the text is a mismatched two-past counterfactual, the acting process must forget this fact. Instead, to heighten the feeling of liveness—which would be that human beings are improvising life—the actor, however, must (whether un-, sub-, or consciously) reimagine the text's counterfactual conditions as a "Might" Counterfactual, as described by Keith DeRose.[18]

The two-past mismatched counterfactual is what is inherent in the dramatic text; a *one-past counterfactual* is (un-, sub-, or consciously) used by the actor to reformulate the dramatic text into a textual script used for acting. The actor, then, needs—to perform liveness—to reimagine Hamlet as the following (via Ippolito) one-past counterfactual (i.e., change the tense of the projections from past perfect to present tense),[19] combining this one-past counterfactual with a "Might" Counterfactual (via DeRose):

> (1) *If* it *were* the case that a brilliant young prince *was* away at college and were to return home after hearing of his father's death, only to find that his mother and uncle have wed, hearing rumors that his uncle (who is now the King) murdered his father, (2) *then* this brilliant young prince *might* [note the modal "might"] *hatch* a plot to revenge his father's murder.

This reformulation has the same resulting *effect* of remembering to forget, but it has the advantage of allowing the actor to *actively* concentrate on something specific (i.e., the specific counterfactual), rather than trying to forget something that the actor already knows (i.e., to unlearn knowledge). While not the sole method for achieving the illusion of "liveness," this reformulation of the text's counterfactual conditions explains the (essentially, subconscious) process that a successful actor undertakes to perform something that appears (to the audience) to be "live"—as though the character were *improvising* his or her life.

Historicizing an Event and/or Object

The history play, in particular, can be thought about to wrap up some final thoughts. In general, on the stage, history makes for a bizarre *event*. I italicize "event" because thinking about once-occurring factual events that are presented on stage multiple times is precisely why plays that invoke history are *weird*. Plays, whether history plays or those that are simply rooted to history, become *twice-told (or more) events*. A history play, or a play that invokes historical events, is generally based upon a set of distinct facts, often about an object and/or an event. Outside of those, usually quite limited number of distinct facts (dates, names, such and such events, etc.), most of the truthfulness of a play comes from a set of subsumed properties that are not (necessarily) *true*, but display, rather, truthfulness. For example, Fernando Arrabal's *Guernica* (1959) is a play that refers to a painting by Pablo Picasso, which, in turn, refers to the bombings of the Basque town of Guernica by the German Nazis and Italian fascists, at the behest of Spanish nationalists. There is nothing that is *true*, per se, about Arrabal's characters or what they say (i.e., they are not historical facts), as they are an abstraction of an abstraction of history. However, there is something *truthful* in their pronouncement of the absurd situation in the actual bombing of Guernica.

In theatre, in general, *plays are tethered to points of correspondence with human nature, whereas history plays are tethered to points of correspondence with distinct facts*. Coherence in a history play is dependent upon the portrayal of human nature, and this is, ultimately, how (a form of) truth is conveyed. However, in the coherence of a history play—in between the lines of historical fact—the history play exposes one of the integral elements that separates theatre from other art forms: that much of the art of theatre is what is not a part of the art itself. That is, the text and the historical facts (of a history play) correspond with the art itself and the world outside of the play. However, what makes the performance portray truth

108 BETWEEN THE LINES

are all of the things that are not specified in the text or in history. There are *distinct* facts that can be derived by the text, but these do not make for theatre (or a performance). The performance is drawn out by the actors and directors and other designers to figure out what is *subsumed within* due to these facts. What a history play does and does not contain in of itself helps differentiate it from other types of theatre, while also creating creative constraints for an actor trying to connect with a character.

6

Subsumption in Theatre

The Question of Lady Bracknell's Nose and Offstage Characters

There are many objects in the theatre that exist explicitly, some of them being quite famous: Yorick's skull (in Shakespeare's *Hamlet*); the dead tree on a country road (in the first act in Beckett's *Waiting for Godot*); a park bench (in Albee's *The Zoo Story*); and a bloody goat (in Albee's *The Goat*). There are also many objects in the theatre whose questionable existences are the subject of our attention: Godot (in *Waiting for Godot*); George and Martha's "son" (in Edward Albee's *Who's Afraid of Virginia Woolf?*); and who or what is on the other end of the dumb waiter (in Harold Pinter's *The Dumb Waiter*). But what about those objects that *exist*, if you will, somewhere in between those two poles? Where on this spectrum, then, can we place, say, Lady Bracknell's nose? Surely, Lady Bracknell *ought* to have a nose, correct? But *where* is her nose in Oscar Wilde's play *The Importance of Being Earnest* (1895)?

David Friedell (2018) has recently discussed the relationship between intrinsic and extrinsic properties of art, specifically in music. Friedell claims that normative social rules dictate who can change the intrinsic or extrinsic properties of a piece of music. I claim that in (text-based) theatre—as a particular art form—the dividing line between intrinsic and extrinsic properties of a play is sometimes tenuous. This tenuousness is due to a play's bifurcated existence as a dramatic text and as (many) theatrical performance(s).

Between the Lines. Michael Y. Bennett, Oxford University Press. © Oxford University Press 2024.
DOI: 10.1093/9780197691700.003.0007

110 BETWEEN THE LINES

David Friedell (2018) claims that contingent social practices dictate who can change a musical work. This claim appears to be vital for understanding many other art forms (broadly defined) in addition to music. Friedell uses examples from other artistic media to strengthen his claim: "In so many cases—paintings, sculptures, tables, buildings, and so on—social practices do not, and ostensibly cannot, prevent individuals from changing an object's intrinsic properties. Social practices, however, commonly prevent individuals from changing normative and extrinsic properties of objects" (Friedell 2018: 816). However, I claim that in (text-based) theatre—as a particular art form—the dividing line between intrinsic and extrinsic properties of a play is sometimes tenuous. This tenuousness is due to a play's bifurcated existence as (1) a dramatic text and (2) (many) theatrical performance(s). Somewhat counterintuitively, some (extratextual) extrinsic properties of a dramatic text become intrinsic in performance(s) while some intrinsic properties of a dramatic text become extrinsic in performance(s).

Why Friedell Cannot Change Bruckner's *Eighth Symphony*

In response to Musical Platonists' claim that a change in a musical work would just create a new musical work of the same name, David Friedell points out that even if one were to accept the position held by Guy Rohrbaugh (2003; in Friedell) and Simon Evnine (2009, 2016; in Friedell) that a musical work can intrinsically change, another issue still persists. Friedell poses the following question: Why can't *he* (i.e., David Friedell) make a change to certain musical works? Friedell answers this question by claiming that while musical works can change, due to contingent social practices, only Bruckner can change his own *Eighth Symphony* (as Bruckner wrote the symphony in 1887 and changed it in 1890) while Friedell cannot:

SUBSUMPTION IN THEATRE 111

Rules, granted normative significance by social practices, govern how musical works should be performed. Different rules may apply to a work at different times. These normative changes explain how works change. When works do not change, such as when I fail to revise Bruckner's symphony, it is because social practices do not allow change to happen. . . . Consequently, my view occupies a middle ground. Like Rohrbaugh and Evnine, I preserve the intuitive ways in which musical works change. There is only one Bruckner's *Eighth Symphony*. Bruckner changed it. He didn't compose a new work in 1890. In a move that is friendly to Platonists, however, I deny that such changes alter intrinsic properties of musical works. Changes to how works should be performed alter only their extrinsic properties. This idea promises a unified solution to the revision puzzle for artifacts beyond music. Changes to a symphony's notes, a game's rules, a novel's words, and a word's spelling are all, on my view, socially determined normative changes to the extrinsic properties of these artifacts. (Friedell 2018: 807)

Similarly, in line with Friedell's stance, in a theatrical performance, changes to words and phrases, changes to the set and lighting, and changes aligned with the overall interpretation of a play would all be considered "socially determined normative changes to the extrinsic properties" of a play.

In the most general sense, what Friedell says about socially determined practices can also be true of theatre. Directors, with or without permission, *do* often make small changes to the dramatic text for a theatrical performance. Directors, however, cannot change whom the play is attributed to, though. As Friedell notes, "Any vandal with a jackhammer can change a road's surface. Given our social practices, only a select few can change a road's speed limit. I can bend my fork but cannot change the socially determined fact that it is proper to put it to the left of my plate" (Friedell 2018). According to Friedell's position, then, small changes to the

112 BETWEEN THE LINES

text by a director, as in our example above, would change only the extrinsic properties of a play. In Friedell's view, normative social rules dictate that only the playwright can make a change to the intrinsic properties of a play.

Problems with Intrinsic-Extrinsic Properties in Theatre

Friedell cites David Lewis's description of the difference between intrinsic and extrinsic properties to delineate his own claims: "[David Lewis] writes, 'A thing has its intrinsic properties in virtue of the way that thing itself, and nothing else, is.' Properties that are not intrinsic are extrinsic. *Has-a-screen* and *has-mass* are intrinsic properties of my laptop computer. *In-a-café* and *belongs-to-me* are some of its extrinsic properties. On my view, *has-a-sound-structure*, *has-lyrics*, *has-a-movement*, and *has-a-verse* are extrinsic properties of musical works. These are properties works have not just in virtue of the way they are. Works have these properties in virtue of the way their performance rules are" (Friedell 2018). Taking Oscar Wilde's play *The Importance of Being Earnest*, as an example, and using Lewis-via-Friedell's distinction between intrinsic and extrinsic properties, therefore, every word, utterance, gesture, and action of Lady Bracknell specified in the dramatic text is intrinsic to both *The Importance of Being Earnest* and to the character of Lady Bracknell.

However, the extrinsic and intrinsic properties of a play are somewhat porous. Wilde's *The Importance of Being Earnest* has a long performance history. Most notably and relevant to this chapter, the character of Lady Bracknell has often been played in drag (i.e., performed by a male actor) due to Lady Bracknell's domineering personality. A recent incarnation of Lady Bracknell in drag was on Broadway in 2011, with Brian Bedford playing Lady Bracknell. As stated by *The New York Times*' theatre critic, Charles Isherwood, "This magnificent gorgon, 'a monster, without being a

SUBSUMPTION IN THEATRE   113

myth,' as the horrified Jack describes her at one point, has perhaps never been more imperious, more indomitable—or more delectably entertaining—than in Mr. Bedford's brilliant portrayal.... Mr. Bedford's stiff posture and serene bustling suggest a woman bearing her rectitude like a suit of armor and her trials with the surety of the righteous" (Isherwood).

The idea here is that Bedford's portrayal changed the extrinsic properties of Lady Bracknell. With Bedford making this extrinsic change, which allows audiences and readers to understand more about the character of Lady Bracknell *now*, in some ways, Bedford also changed how *future* audiences and scholars and actors view the intrinsic nature of Lady Bracknell. Given that the text contains the intrinsic properties of a piece of theatre while also suggesting the permissible or nonpermissible extrinsic properties allowed in its performance, this portrayal highlights how the textual Lady Bracknell (the intrinsic Lady Bracknell) is now understood to be more monstrous and domineering than she had been prior to Bedford's performance. Here, not only does Bedford's portrayal make a change, but Isherwood's commentary on the performance also changes our perception of the intrinsic properties of the play. In addition, both Bedford's portrayal and Isherwood's commentary affect future performances and artistic choices that will be made surrounding not only the portrayal of Lady Bracknell but also the play as a whole. Likewise, Friedell can change *The Importance of Being Earnest* simply by putting on/being a part of a production or by writing a performance review or an interpretation of the play.

However, while we can presume that Lady Bracknell *has-a-body* and the *having-of-a-body* is intrinsic to both the play and to Lady Bracknell, the gender and/or sex of the *actor* playing Lady Bracknell is, according to Lewis-via-Friedell's distinction, *extrinsic* to Lady Bracknell and the play. This opens up some further issues. For example, presumably, the character of Lady Bracknell has a nose. And one would presume that *having-a-nose* is intrinsic to Lady Bracknell. However, Lady Bracknell's nose is not mentioned in the play (i.e., Oscar Wilde's dramatic text of *The Importance of Being Earnest*).[1] Does that mean her nose is *extrinsic* to both Lady Bracknell and to the play? Is there a possible world in which Lady Bracknell does *not* have a nose? Does Lady Bracknell's nose have a transworld identity? "To say that there is a transworld identity between A and B is to say that there is some possible world w_1, and some distinct possible world w_2, such that A exists in w_1, and B exists in w_2, and A is identical with B" (Mackie and Jago 2013). For things not specified in the text of a play, say, the identity of Godot (from Samuel Beckett's *Waiting for Godot* [1952]), or whether or not the character of Lady Bracknell employs ten, fifteen, or more than twenty servants, we have a different *type* of trans-world identity: "To say there is trans-*world* identity between possible worlds w_1 and w_2, is to say that both 1) X exists in w_1 and Y exists in w_2, and 2) $w_1 - X = w_2 - Y$. This question is essentially a debate as to whether global information subsequently changes when . . . the local information explicit in the counterfactual conditional (e.g., an offstage character) is substituted with other possible identities within the bounds set forth in the counterfactual conditional" (Bennett 2017: 117–118). And while these questions have their own philosophical import to modal logic, who or whatever Godot is, or changes in the precise number or servants employed by Lady Bracknell, will not change the production of either of these plays.

However, what about those properties that bridge the intrinsic-extrinsic divide, such as whether Lady Bracknell has a nose? Most of the theatrical performance of a dramatic text falls into this intrinsic-extrinsic gray zone. The issue here is not that other pieces of art, especially novels and short stories, refer to things that are not specified in the text, but rather that in theatre, some of those extratextual extrinsic elements in a dramatic text become intrinsic in performance (e.g., Lady Bracknell's nose). And some of those intrinsic properties of Lady Bracknell become extrinsic in performance (e.g., Lady Bracknell's gender and/or sex).

Indeterminate Identity

In claiming that abstract creationism can be committed to indeterminate identity, David Friedell (2020) suggests that whether fictional realism entails there is indeterminate identity depends upon what fictional characters *are*. In this chapter, I will claim that there is indeterminate identity in fictional characters, suggesting that the case of theatre is important to consider when discussing both indeterminate identity and the ontology of fictional characters. I will do this, then, by considering a specific type of fictional character: the offstage character in theatre. I would like to join this conversation—which, thus far, has mostly focused on largely generic fictional entities—by claiming that examining theatre's most famous offstage character, Godot, in Samuel Beckett's *Waiting for Godot* (1952/1953), presents a somewhat different problem case about indeterminate identity.

In the rest of this chapter, I examine indeterminate identity, *not by asking whether two characters can be identical*, but by claiming that *it is indeterminate as to whether an offstage character can correspond to multiple fictional entities*. With a theatrical performance having a material reality on stage(s)—not just on the page—there is an embodied reality that does, and does not, change with varying performances of the same dramatic text. In short, does the identity of an offstage character matter to the onstage world of the play? Whether or not the onstage and/or offstage world of the play changes, in what ways does the fact that an offstage character has an indeterminate identity affect the (onstage) world of the play? To these questions, I defend the claim that there can be indeterminate identity in regard to fictional characters, certainly, at least, when this affects fictional characters that are offstage with respect to a theatrical onstage performance.

I will first turn to David Friedell's (2019) recent contribution to the conversation surrounding indeterminate identity to lay out the current debate. Turning to Schnieder and von Solodkoff's nursery rhyme, *Bah-Tale* (2009), Friedell discusses the ways in which abstract creationism can be committed to the existence of indeterminate identity. To address this conversation indirectly, I will introduce the case of Godot from Samuel Beckett's *Waiting for Godot* to change the conversation to claim that it is indeterminate whether a single offstage character can correspond to multiple fictional entities and fictional identities. Next, I will examine how thinking about theatre as a specific art form raises three questions about indeterminate identity. After that, I will address some possible responses that Platonists and abstract creationists may have to my claims. Then, with those possible responses addressed, I will attempt to answer the three questions I posed earlier, finally followed by a short conclusion.

Friedell (2020) begins his critique of Everett's (2005) rejection of fictional realism with Schnieder and von Solodkoff's *Bah-Tale*, which is based upon one of Everett's stories:

Bah-Tale
There once was a man called Bahrooh
There once was a man called Bahraah
But nobody knew if Bahraah was Bahrooh
Or if they were actually two (Schnieder and von Solodkoff 2009: 139)

Contra Everett (2005), Woodward (2017) concludes that while it may be indeterminate to assess whether Bahrooh and Bahraah are identical, this is a matter of indeterminate *reference*—not a question of indeterminate identity. Friedell (2019) admires Woodward's line of thought, but wishes that Woodward explained the ontology of fictional characters. Friedell (2019) concludes that while Platonism may avoid positing indeterminate identity, abstract creationism—and certainly the version put forth by Evnine (2016)—is committed to indeterminate identity.

SUBSUMPTION IN THEATRE 117

According to Friedell (2019), Woodward's (2017) claim—that indeterminate identity does not exist, but (to return to *Bah-Tale*) that "Bahrooh" and "Bahraah" are indeterminate references—does not take into account the ontology of fictional characters. Friedell (2019) suggests that a Platonist, who believes in abstract objects that are eternal and that "a character is a set of all the properties that are true of a character in the fiction," can accommodate Woodward's (2017) conclusion that there is only indeterminate reference. To Friedell (2019), it is unclear whether one is referring to a character that is Bahrooh-ish, Bahraah-ish, or both Bahrooh-ish and Bahraah-ish, which makes a case for indeterminate reference.

Friedell (2019) suggests that, if abstract creationism is true, there is such a thing as indeterminate identity. Friedell suggests that thinking through Evnine (2016) can help demonstrate how indeterminate identity exists. Friedell plays off of the idea that in the morning, someone wrote a story, *Cah-Tale Part 1*, which, in its entirety reads, "There once was a woman called Cahrooh"; then, in the evening, this same person wrote a sequel, called *Cah-Tale Part 2*, which reads, "There once was a woman called Cahraah / But nobody knew if Cahraah was Cahrooh / Or if they were actually two." In Friedell's (2019) eyes, Evnine (2016) would suggest that since it is indeterminate whether Cahraah from the morning is the same as from the evening that it is also indeterminate whether Cahraah is identical to Cahrooh.

Godot-Tale

I would like to add a new nursery rhyme to this conversation, based upon Samuel Beckett's (1952 French/1954 English) play *Waiting for Godot*, famously about two tramps who wait for a man named Godot, who never shows up. I use this example because while Godot is central to the play, his offstage actions and existence (which are,

118 BETWEEN THE LINES

largely, unknown) do not affect the onstage action. Therefore, does it matter who Godot is?

This example presents a slightly different problem case about indeterminate identity. Instead of asking whether two characters can be identical, the case of Godot and the offstage character in theatre raises a problem where a single fictional character that has properties associated with it can be satisfied by two (or more) different fictional entities and/or different fictional identities. That is, it is indeterminate to which, or to how many, identities Godot can correspond. Here, *Godot-Tale* is meant to be a pithy summary of Beckett's *Waiting for Godot* (i.e., "Godot" in *Godot-Tale* refers to the same fictional character as in Beckett's play):

> *Godot-Tale*
> There once was a white-bearded man named Godot.
> But nobody knew if he was God,
> Or if he was Hope,
> Or if those two were one in the same.
> But everyone knew that whatever he was,
> They just knew that Godot never came.

According to Pinillos (2003), "alleged cases [of split indeterminate identity (SII)] arise when there are objects x, y, and z such that it is indeterminate that x=y, indeterminate that x=z, but (determinate that) y≠z" (35). Based upon some common readings and understandings of *Waiting for Godot* (where theatre critics have suggested that Godot is God or Godot is Hope), we can suggest that if x = Godot, y = God, and z = Hope, then, in this case, it is indeterminate that Godot = God and indeterminate that Godot = Hope. However, in this situation, y *may* equal z (i.e., God may equal Hope), but not *necessarily*. It is not certain, therefore, in this case, whether Godot has an SII, or this is simply a case of uncertainty.

However, to complicate this line of reasoning, outside of the fact that we know from the play that Godot *is a man* and *has a white beard*, there is a wide range of possible identities that can satisfy to whom Godot corresponds. Using an example found in Bennett (2017), Godot could correspond to either A or B, where A = Uncle Sam, or B = Santa Claus. Here, let us use Pinillos's (2003) above formulation: x = Godot, y = Uncle Sam, and z = Santa Claus. In this situation, unlike above, it is determinate that y ≠ z (i.e., Uncle Sam ≠ Santa Claus). In this situation, then, Godot has an SII.

Theatrical Performance

Fictional characters exist in fictional worlds; in theatre, as I suggest in Bennett (2017), we see both a fictional world presented in a performance but also variations of this fictional world in various performances. Different actors and directors and designers imagine and embody (somewhat) different worlds, with actors even embodying different fictional characters, as long as characters across performances abide by the rules set out in the dramatic text. The *theatrical* offstage character complicates conversations surrounding fictional entities that are merely referred to in ways that cannot be adequately explored in, say, thinking about a novel. I suggest the importance of considering theatre as a specific art form when thinking about fictional characters and entities. That is, in a novel, stemming from the words on the page, everything works within the imagination, and different imaginings of different characters are central to the reading process of fiction.

This issue of embodying different fictional characters is explored all the time in casting a theatrical production. In some ways, thinking about theatre as a whole, the very fact that different human actors can satisfy the same roles to play the same theatrical character, even if well-defined by a number of properties that are unique to the theatrical character, gets to the heart of the importance of studying theatrical characters in relation to these issues of indeterminate identity and the ontology of fictional characters.

120 BETWEEN THE LINES

The difference between an offstage character versus an onstage character is that while different human actors can satisfy the same onstage fictional character in different ways, the onstage world of the play does not change if we imagine different human bodies embodying an offstage character. With the case of an offstage character, the question arises whether the onstage and/or offstage world of the play changes, and, in turn, if that affects the (onstage) world of the play. Three questions, therefore, must be raised:

Given the following,
  if Director A thinks "Godot is God"
  if Director B thinks "Godot is Hope"
  if Director C thinks "Godot is God *and* is Hope"
  if Director D thinks "Godot is God, but is *not* Hope"
  if Director E thinks "Godot is *not* God, but is Hope"
  if Director F thinks "Godot is Uncle Sam"
  and if Director G thinks "Godot is Santa Claus"
then

1. Do the performances by Directors A–G all produce the same onstage reality, or does the change in the identity of the offstage character ensure that the fictional world of the play is different and, therefore, the play/performance is necessarily different?
2. How does, or does (*merely*) thinking about who Godot is affect indeterminate identity?
3. How is Godot related to the fictional world of the play, and vice versa, how is the fictional world of the play related to Godot?

Because even though numerous fictional entities/identities can satisfy who Godot refers to, the onstage world of the play does not (necessarily) change, my short answer is that Godot presents a case of indeterminate identity. I will attempt to answer these three questions one at a time, though, after I first address some possible responses that Platonists and abstract creationists may raise.

Possible Responses by Platonists and Abstract Creationists

What might a Platonist say about the indeterminacy of Godot? Thinking about a fictional character as a set of all of its properties, we do, in fact, have two properties associated with the Godot: *is-white-bearded* and *is-male*. While excluding many, many possible fictional characters, those two properties certainly do not preclude that many; however, many Platonists might suggest that there is a *character* that only has those two properties. The Platonist may reply that the sameness relation between that set and other fictional characters is a relation weaker than identity (Castañeda 1989).

The issue at hand here, however, in the case of Godot, is whether there are *enough* (and enough sufficient) properties for Godot to correspond to a determinate identity. What we do not know, importantly, is how many things have these two properties. In the case of Godot, in either of these situations—one in which Godot corresponds to Uncle Sam and one in which Godot corresponds to Santa Claus—the onstage world of the play is exactly the same, for whether Godot corresponds to A or B does not affect the action of the play. However, the offstage world(s) would appear to be different. For example, if it were the case that Godot had a female partner, the partner of Uncle Sam would be different than the partner of Santa Claus. And, to go on, if Uncle Sam and his partner and Santa Claus and his partner had (biological) children, the children that Uncle Sam would produce would definitely be different than the children that Santa Claus would produce. And, then, it would seem to be the case that the children produced may have different friends and associates, and the butterfly effect can go on from there, spawning quite different (offstage) worlds of the play.

122　BETWEEN THE LINES

Of course, none of this affects the onstage world of the play. And that is the exact point: Godot really is an indeterminate identity, if this is the case.

What might an abstract creationist say about the indeterminacy of Godot? Evnine (2016), via Friedell (2019), maintains that (for abstract creationists) authors create characters: "Just as Evnine thinks we must intend to create a fictional character in order to create one, he thinks we must intend to create a watch in order to create one" (Friedell 2020: 5). What would the case of Godot mean for the abstract creationists who are intentionalists?[2]

However, while it is clear that Beckett intended to create the character, Godot—and thus it would follow that there is, in fact, a fictional character, Godot—when asked, Samuel Beckett famously remarked, "If I knew what Godot was, then I would have said so" (Levy 1956: 74–75). I do not think—though I could easily be wrong—that the (intentional) abstract creationism, however, currently has a precise answer to account for an intention that is either vague or without specification.

Returning to the Three Questions

So let us now return to the three questions posed earlier in this essay. I will address them, one at a time.

1. Do the performances by Directors A–G all produce the same onstage reality, or does the change in the identity of the offstage character ensure that the fictional world of the play is different and therefore the play/performance is necessarily different?

Thinking about to whom/what Godot corresponds certainly *can* change the onstage world of the play: for example, thinking about Godot as God (who never comes) can produce a bleak world onstage, with cooler lighting and a more destitute-looking set, whereas maybe thinking about Godot as something like a person who is an

SUBSUMPTION IN THEATRE 123

unhelpful crutch to lean on might produce a world onstage that is filled with warmer-hued and brighter lighting and a less-destitute-looking set. However, this is not the *necessary* conclusion. After all, it is not even necessary to even think about who Godot is; Samuel Beckett did a pretty good job with the play without knowing who Godot is, either.

This idea leads to our second question, as thinking about whether we even need to think about Godot's identity is vital:

2. How does, or does, (*merely*) thinking about who Godot is affect indeterminate identity?

In many ways, and certainly in a situation as with an offstage character like Godot, Hans-Georg Gadamer's (1960) notion that one need not take into account the intention of the author when reading and/or interpreting fiction is quite relevant. While the author's intention does not matter (via Gadamer), in a case like Godot, to the audience, it may not matter what the intentions of the director, actors, designers, and so on are, either, for the onstage actions need not change whatsoever, whether it is even thought about who Godot is.

Again, the question of Godot's identity, whether it is thought about indeterminately, or in a single performance, is quite specified in the minds of the whole cast and crew, does not necessarily translate to the audience. Therefore, because of this, the world of the play comes to the forefront in the third question:

3. How is Godot related to the fictional world of the play, and vice versa, how is the fictional world of the play related to Godot?

In this question about the relation of Godot to the world of the play, again, the answer is simply, it *can*, but does *not necessarily* change the fictional world of the play.

It is in this idea of *it can, but not necessarily* that the indeterminate identity of offstage characters in the theatre rests. That is, conceiving the offstage character of Godot corresponding to

124 BETWEEN THE LINES

different identities may appropriately change the world of the play, but it may not either. If the world of the play *always* changed in situations where Godot corresponded to different identities, then one might be at least able to assert that "Godot" refers to a vague referent. However, since the world of the play *does not have to change* with Godot corresponding to different identities, then it appears as though the identity, at least for Godot in Beckett's *Waiting for Godot*, is indeterminate.[3]

7

Truthfulness in Theatre

Imagined Objects and Actors and Acting

What does it mean for something to be *truthful* in the theatre? Truthful properties and truthfulness in the theatre are types of subsumed properties and are *not true by necessity*, and, in fact, they *could be false*. But—and here's the key—truthful properties say something true about human nature and/or the human experience.

For example, the casting of a role to play a theatrical character can be a tricky task. The dramatic text (in text-based theatre) creates the *dos* and *don'ts* for performance, both through stage directions and what the characters say (and, sometimes explicitly and sometimes implicitly, do). However, most of the art of theatre is not specified in the dramatic text, as the doing of theatre— the enacted embodiment of a play—is where the fleshing out of a theatrical artistic idea happens. A theatrical character is the sum total of his or her actions and statements (Bennett 2017), but an embodied character played by an actor also has a whole host of properties that are either made explicit (or are implicit or are not even mentioned) in the text. For the director, the question of whom to cast and how that actor should embody that character becomes problematic in the face of *any* type and/or amount of deviation (even in the slightest) from the dramatic text. That is, the logic of casting and acting dictates that the actor cannot embody or act the opposite way of anything that is explicitly stated in the dramatic text. Along these lines, I have previously suggested that there is something of a "kernel" of a character that is *necessarily true* in all possible productions (2017: 36–37). Even granting my previous

Between the Lines. Michael Y. Bennett, Oxford University Press. © Oxford University Press 2024.
DOI: 10.1093/9780197691700.003.0008

126 BETWEEN THE LINES

claim, though, two problems arise: (1) How are we to understand the properties of theatrical characters that are not specified and/or not even implied in the text? (2) How can a director ever justify cross-casting (e.g., gender, race, age, etc.)?

These two questions get to the very heart of "who is" a theatrical character, which is central to the task of interpretation. Therefore, for example, asking "Who is Hamlet?" is a question that has, for centuries, been asked and never fully (or satisfactorily) been definitively answered. What if, rather, we ask, "Who *cannot* be Hamlet?" By thinking about acting and the character through the concepts of *subsumption* and *distinctness* (as used in philosophical semantics), this chapter is not trying to define a theatrical character by way of the negative. What asking this question does, rather, is create a spectrum where "Who *is* Hamlet?" and "Who *cannot be* Hamlet?" are the two poles that contain distinct properties (that either distinctly define who Hamlet is or are properties that are distinctly *not*-Hamlet). But these two poles are less of the concern of this essay, as between these poles (i.e., on this spectrum), however, are, I claim, all of the *subsumed properties* within the character of Hamlet. Investigating the subsumed properties of a character helps thread the needle between something that is necessarily *true* versus something that is *truthful*.

Thinking about a character's distinct properties and their subsumed properties in the dramatic text, then, offers the director and actor an entirely new way to cast and embody a character, without thinking as much about necessary strict adhesion to a dramatic text. That is not to say anything goes (or should go) in theatre and is allowable and/or truthful to the dramatic text, but that thinking about distinctness and subsumption helps thread the needle between something that is necessarily true versus something truthful, if you will, which mimics the difference between a fictional character being true versus a fictional character embodying something truthful. In the play, as mentioned earlier in the Introduction, *The Importance of Being Earnest*, it is *not true* that Lady Bracknell has a male body, but when played by a male actor, this embodiment says something *truthful* about Lady Bracknell.

Instead of using subsumption to only describe constituent parts of a thing, I will attempt to demonstrate how subsumption can also be useful to describe properties of a thing (at least, in theatre). While it is rather clear how a grain of sand is subsumed within a heap of sand (i.e., a heap of sand is made up of constituent grains of sands), I claim that at least in the case of theatrical characters, properties can be subsumed within a dramatic text. After that, I will introduce how thinking about "Who cannot be Hamlet?" through the concepts of subsumption and distinctness can help better our understanding of casting and theatrical performance when considering the question of Hamlet's madness. Then, I will revisit two examples from the previous chapter (i.e., Chapter 6) to discuss two possible objections that may be raised: (1) offstage characters and the case of Godot from Samuel Beckett's *Waiting for Godot* and (2) cross-casting and the case of cross-gender casting Lady Bracknell from Oscar Wilde's *The Importance of Being Earnest*.

Subsumption of Properties: Interpretation and Sane, South-by-Southeast?

Expanding the usage of two concepts from philosophical semantics, *subsumption* and *distinctness*, will help us better understand how to cast a character and the art of acting. Subsumption, again, refers to the idea that larger, if you will, objects and statements have smaller, if you will, parts subsumed within. Distinctness, again, refers to the idea that when objects/statements are unique, they do not overlap. Turning to our subject at hand, theatre, let us think through the character of Hamlet and what is distinct (specifically stated and unique) and what properties are subsumed within the dramatic text (not stated, nor unique, but are a part of the character). "Who is Hamlet?" asks what properties are distinct properties about

128 BETWEEN THE LINES

Hamlet, whereas "Who cannot be Hamlet?" in a sense raises the same question but forces us to examine what is not stated, and what is subsumed by those distinct properties that make Hamlet Hamlet. There is what Hamlet does and says in the dramatic text and then there is a whole extra layer of properties and actions subsumed by those distinct statements and actions found in the text. So now let us think about the question, "Who cannot be Hamlet?"

We have a few statements, for example, about Hamlet—from Hamlet himself—about his possibly "mad" state of mind: (1) to Guildenstern, "I am mad north-by-north-west" (II. ii. 360.); (2) to Horatio, he "put[s] an antic disposition on" (I. v. 172); and (3) to his mother, Gertrude, "I essentially am not in madness / But mad in craft" (III. iv. 187–198.). In thinking about the age-old question of whether Hamlet is mad and/or feigns madness, let us think about distinct and subsumed properties both in thinking about who Hamlet is and who Hamlet cannot be. These properties will not necessarily answer this question over Hamlet's madness, but they will help develop a performance score for the actor based upon how they interpret his madness, thereby figuring out what needs to be made distinct and/or subsumed in the embodied portrayal.

"Madness" is defined as "Insanity; mental illness or impairment, esp. of a severe kind; (later *esp.*) psychosis; an instance of this" (*OED*). "Psychosis," to go further, according to the American Psychiatric Association and the World Health Organization, is characterized by hallucinations and/or delusions (Arciniegas 2015). Often in acting we see darting eyes or rapid speech or manic demonstrative movements as a sign of psychosis or madness, but these are often comorbid symptoms. I think of Claire Danes's excellent portrayal of a character with bipolar mania in *Homeland*, but while her character has temporary bouts of mania as an expression of her illness, she *is not* "insane," nor is someone who is bipolar, as they suffer *temporary* bouts of psychosis, but those are temporary states versus a permanent state of being, which is what is generally implied by madness, especially in *Hamlet*. That is, while these symptoms may not be present in the text as distinct properties tied to Hamlet, these symptoms are subsumed by the larger idea of mental illness, but not necessarily by the idea of psychosis. An actor might subsume bits of mania to make a pronounced distinct feature of insanity or psychosis rapid speech, which is a distinct feature of mania, but does not suggest that someone is necessarily *insane*. How does one, then, see an actor have delusions? That is, what are some distinct properties of a delusion and/or what is subsumed within a delusion (e.g., a delusion can easily be a delusion of grandiosity, and how does, or how would, one show that?)?

Should an actor want to portray a "mad" Hamlet, an actor needs to simultaneously think what madness is, and what madness cannot be. This is something close to Jean-Paul Sartre's idea of "bad faith," such as the waiter in the café that simultaneously knows he is a waiter and is not a waiter. However, this idea is less tied to who a person is in the metaphysical sense, but more about how an actor portrays properties that are subsumed by those distinct properties and actions specified in the text. And asking the question, what is not madness produces a more truthful portrayal than thinking about actions associated with madness.

So if we now apply this to the actor playing Hamlet, by thinking about who Hamlet is and is not, and also thinking about subsumption and distinctness, we have list of possible properties that an either "craft"-y Hamlet or a "mad" Hamlet may possess. So if madness is defined as "insanity," then what madness is not is "sanity" ("The condition of being sane; soundness of mind; mental health" [*OED*]). How does one portray sanity? Let us think about how "soundness" is defined as "Firmness, solidity; freedom from weakness, defect, or damage; goodness of condition or repair" and "Thoroughness, completeness" (*OED*). Basically, an actor who can demonstrate a weak or defective mind that is lacking in thoroughness and completeness can demonstrate insanity and/or "delusions" (i.e., experiencing an objective reality in a false manner) (*OED*). So based upon one interpretation of the character, Hamlet, options

130 BETWEEN THE LINES

that can demonstrate a "mad" Hamlet are both/either physical and/or verbal: stops and starts, unevenness, irregular pacing, and non-linearity and/or incompleteness. Or, based upon the opposite inter-pretation, the actor who can demonstrate fluidity, evenness, regular pacing, linearity, and/or completeness away from those he may want to feign madness in front of can demonstrate sanity, thereby producing a Hamlet that is only mad "in craft."

These properties that an actor may try to embody when playing Hamlet are not necessarily uniquely derived through thinking about who Hamlet is and is not, as other acting techniques could certainly arrive at these same conclusions. However, in matter of interpretation, thinking who Hamlet is not, and, subsequently, what can be subsumed within the character Hamlet, does produce a different method to get produce *truthfulness*.

Possible Objection 1: Offstage Characters

Building off of the previous chapter's exploration of indeterminate identity, the objection(s) that an offstage character has an *indeterminate identity*, or is simply is an *indeterminate reference* or even more simply is a *vague reference*, challenges both of the questions: "Who is Hamlet?" and "Who cannot be Hamlet?" Our same problem case exists of our offstage character, Godot, from Samuel Beckett's *Waiting for Godot* (1952 French/1954 English), who only has two stated properties in the play: *is-white-bearded* and *is-male*. "Who is Godot?" or "Who cannot be Godot?" are problematic questions be-cause the identity of Godot, even when thinking about wildly dif-ferent identities, will not affect that onstage world of the play.

Since, as we explored in the last chapter, it does not matter who an offstage character is for the onstage world of the play—as the identity of an offstage character either (1) has indeterminate iden-tity, (2) is an indeterminate reference, or simply (3) is a vague reference—because whoever the offstage character is (or is not)

TRUTHFULNESS IN THEATRE   131

does not affect the onstage world of the play—one may argue that my claims fall apart. Given that recent argumentation about indeterminacy related to fictional characters has been discussed through Platonism and abstract creationism,[1] I will think about two objections: one that Platonists raise and one that abstract creationists may raise.

First, what might a Platonist say about who can or cannot be Godot? Thinking about a fictional character as a set of all of its properties, we do, in fact, have two properties associated with Godot: *is-white-bearded* and *is-male*. However, those two properties, while excluding many, many possible fictional characters, certainly does not preclude that many, though many Platonists might suggest that there is a *character* that only has those two properties. The Platonist may reply that the sameness relation between that set and other fictional characters is a relation weaker than identity.[2]

Second, what might an abstract creationist say about who can be or not be Godot? Evnine (2016), via Friedell (2020), maintains that (for abstract creationists) authors create characters: "Just as Evnine thinks we must intend to create a fictional character in order to create one, he thinks we must intend to create a watch in order to create one" (Friedell 2020: 5). What would the case of Godot mean for abstract creationists who are intentionalists?[3]

The issue at hand here in the case of Godot, however, is whether there are *enough* (and enough sufficient) properties for Godot to correspond to a determinate identity. What we do *not* know, importantly, is how many things have these two properties. In the case of Godot, in either of these situations—for example, one in which Godot corresponds to Uncle Sam and one in which Godot corresponds to Santa Claus (Bennett 2017: 117)—the onstage world of the play is exactly the same, for whether Godot corresponds to A or B does not affect the action of the play. However, the off-stage world(s) would appear to be different, as discussed earlier in Chapter 6. At least according to an earlier assertion of mine, is that

132　BETWEEN THE LINES

the exact point of *Waiting for Godot* is that Godot does not matter at all for the play, and that is the entire so-called *meaning* behind the play, that Vladimir and Estragon do not need a savior like Godot, whomever that savior could be, because all they need, and what they have, is each other (Bennett 2011: 49–51).

Possible Objection 2: Cross-Gender Casting and Lady Bracknell's Nose

The other possible objection that may arise is when a theatrical character is cross-casted, either cross-gender or cross-race casting being the two most common types of cross-casting. One famous example of cross-gender casting outside of Shakespearean and ancient Greek/Roman theatre, both of which made wide use of cross-gender casting, is the character of Lady Bracknell, who is often played by a male actor, in productions of Oscar Wilde's *The Importance of Being Earnest* (1895). One may raise the objection that since theatre accommodates cross-casting, that thinking about who a character is not becomes problematic in the face of casting practices.

This issue of embodying different fictional characters is explored all of the time in casting a theatrical production. In some ways, thinking about theatre as a whole, the very fact that different human actors can satisfy the same roles to play the same theatrical character, even if well-defined by a number of properties that are unique to the theatrical character, gets to the heart of the importance of studying theatrical characters in relation to these issues of indeterminate identity and the ontology of fictional characters. The difference between an offstage character versus a character onstage is that while different human actors can satisfy the same onstage fictional character in different ways, the onstage world of the play does not change if we imagine different human bodies embodying an offstage character. With the case of an offstage character, the

TRUTHFULNESS IN THEATRE   133

question arises whether the onstage and/or offstage world of the play changes and, in turn, if that affects the (onstage) world of the play. Phillip B. Zarrilli has suggested that "the actor enacts a specific performance score" and it is the actor's body that "is a site through which representation as a well as experience are generated for both self and other" (2004: 664). For Zarrilli, once the performance score is created, "the actor is inhabiting and embodying a score through which he appears to act in a world" so that, for example, when the actor breathes, it appears to be the character breathing (2004: 664–665).[4]

But the idea here is that the so-called performance score is based upon a *body* cast for that role, but a role where the unwritten characteristics of the character are subsumed in *that* body. The intellectual thrust in thinking about subsumption in acting and theatre, as a whole, is that what is not specified in the dramatic text can be argued to be subsumed in the dramatic text. Why does this matter? For this chapter, though, it is not that the intrinsic nature of who Lady Bracknell is that is important (as was important in Chapter 6), but that a male body more easily subsumes Lady Bracknell's "imperious" and "indomitable" nature.

That is, it not only becomes only permissible to cross-gender cast the role of Lady Bracknell, but the male body offers (in general) *distinct* characteristics from the female body that can, then, be *subsumed* in the portrayal of the character. It is not only important for the actor, in that case Brian Bedford, but for others to understand what is distinct in the actor's body and what then either needs to be subsumed by making adjustments and/or cannot be subsumed, and therefore, must understand how to deal with a unique/distinct characteristic, whether or not this characteristic is contradictory, aligned, or just subsumed within the text.

In this case, Lady Bracknell's sex is a distinct property. Her name after all is "Lady Bracknell"; she is the "mother" of Gwendolyn and "aunt" to Algernon. By all accounts, then, her sex as female is a distinct property in the play. This is based upon the explicit content, to

134 BETWEEN THE LINES

go back to Stokke's language. Then there is some implicit content, like Lady Bracknell's nose, which would fall under the category of a subsumed property. Of course, too, that would include Lady Bracknell's hair, her two feet, her left hand, as well as right hand, her internal bodily organs, and so on. However, while it may be distinct that Lady Bracknell is of the female sex, that does not necessarily suggest that because her *sex* is *female* that her gender need be represented, likewise, as such. Here, Lady Bracknell's gender, or at least, through cross-casting, her *gender* as *male* provides a truthful property about Lady Bracknell and her overbearing, alpha male qualities.

Here, I have introduced three questions that an actor and/or director may ask about theatrical characters in an effort to decide what is true about a character and/or truthful about a character: (1) What are the distinct properties of [a character]? (2) What is distinctly *not*-[a character]? and (3) What properties are subsumed within [a character]? Based upon these questions, hopefully, I have demonstrated how artistic choices can be made based upon *interpretation* (e.g., a "mad" Hamlet or a not-"mad" Hamlet) and/or artistic choices can be made based upon *truthfulness* (e.g., having Lady Bracknell portrayed by a male actor).

Imagined Objects: Between Spider Angiomas and Signposts

In terms of understanding and comprehension to commonly viewed concrete objects, what happens when knowledge/information is *unfolding* during an artistic performance? There has been some previous work done regarding updating expectations and/or knowledge as audiences/readers learn new information from an art form (though not much work has been done in regard, specifically, to theatre and performance studies). Writing specifically about reading literature, Tzachi Zamir suggests that it is not necessarily *knowledge* or, by extension, *information* (i.e., that which is either *true* or *false*) that is being learned (in his case, by reading), but what is being learned is, what he terms, *meaningfulness*, how "literature expands lived experience" and justifies one's own beliefs, whether beliefs, justified beliefs, or justified true beliefs.[5] Jerrold Levinson, in *Music in the Moment* (1997),[6] suggests that musical understanding occurs from the listener grasping *small, successive* bits of music; this would be in contrast to the idea that a listener needs to grasp (aurally or intellectually) a piece of music in its entirety. On the other hand, in discussing the understanding of cinema, Noël Carroll—in his article "Performance" (1986)[7] and in his book *The Philosophy of Motion Pictures* (2008)[8]—suggests that the moviegoer (consciously or unconsciously) asks a series of questions that he or she answers as new data from the movie emerge, allowing for the moviegoer to update his or her comprehension. Zamir, Levinson, and Carroll's accounts of updating comprehension (granted, for three different art forms), however, are focused upon *individuals*, who are each individually receiving these art forms.

What happens, then, when other people are introduced into the equation? In *The Art of Theater* (2007), Hamilton discusses at length how people come to an agreement and can describe the same object and/or event. Hamilton extends David Lewis's coordination games to introduce the way that audiences become "*learners*."[9] Audience members, thus, learn to look to the precedence of "salient" features (i.e., features of the performance that stand out).[10] By doing so, audience members can "project" what is going to be "right most of the time."[11] The understanding of a performance is shaped, according to Hamilton, by picking out salient features "reasonably related to her own perspective":[12]

> Spectators do not know in advance *what* they will find. But, crucially, they know that everyone else will be looking *for the same things*. Thus, while spectators are not guaranteed to find exactly and all the same things salient, the thickened concept of common

136 BETWEEN THE LINES

knowledge guarantees the possibility, indeed the likelihood, that they will find roughly the same set of features salient.[13]

Hamilton's notion of picking out salient features and projecting what will happen while knowing that everyone else is doing the same admirably addresses how we agree on discrete facts and situations.

However, even if we "find roughly the same set of features salient," does that mean we *share* the same viewing experience? In Bennett (2021), I discuss how commonly viewed objects can be experienced differently by different audience members, given that differing prior experiences and knowledge bases of the audience members require that audience members seek out different types of information. As stated above, in *The Art of Theater* (2007), James R. Hamilton suggests that by understanding precedence and projecting salient features of the performance—and by understanding that everyone else is doing the same thing—that spectators all come to possess a rough common knowledge of the same events. The work of Hamilton and the work, too, of Jerrold Levinson, Tzachi Zamir, and Noël Carroll all aid in the understanding of a *concrete* object.

The problem with these accounts of understanding, however, is that these accounts assume that all of our knowledge comes from experiencing the same *concrete objects* and *concrete actions*. Of course, concrete events transpire over the course of a theatrical performance, but often, whether consciously, subconsciously, or unconsciously, *a good deal of our experience in theatre happens in our imaginations*. Sometimes, too, our theatrical experience relies on what our imaginations, even, choose to ignore. Thus, we have to ask, What about the uninvestigated spaces of theatrical stages that have not been experienced and/or do not exist, except in the imagination of, say, audience members?

It is not just, for example, offstage characters that are caught in the crosshairs of the imagination of the different viewers; so, too,

TRUTHFULNESS IN THEATRE   137

whether passively or actively, the empty spaces of the stage are often filled in more completely by imagination. Importantly, multiple viewers are all doing this, too:

> The audience both needs to be given and looks for *signposts* and *landmarks* as the play progresses through the landscape the play sets for itself. Landmarks and signposts in the theatre take many forms: props, human actions that happen based upon previous action, passage of time, change of location, following the "unities," stage animals, etc. If the audience is passing through the Tyrones' house over the course of a long day and night, one is looking for signposts that with each passing gulp of the prop— the whiskey—the Tyrone men ought to get and act more and more drunk as the night progresses. The ice cubes rattling in the glass, the swirling of the glass, and the correct hue of the dyed water all give the audience specific landmarks and signposts that the men are getting and *ought* to continue to get more drunk. Of course, the slurring of speech, the variations of intonation, and the increasingly wobbly physical gestures will also serve as signposts and landmarks, as well. The key here, though, is that not all of the signposts and landmarks need to be present to guide us into, and through, the world of the Tyrones; given the richness of our world versus the sparseness of a fictional world (due to the inability to describe and delineate every detail), *not* all of the signposts and landmarks, almost assuredly, will be present. Thus, the stench of whiskey on the breath, the presence of tiny spider angiomas on the skin, profuse sweating, redness in the palms, etc. are not necessary to suggest drunkenness.[14]

We, as audience members, use our imaginations (to various degrees, and somewhere along the passive-active spectrum) to allow ourselves to believe, or at least play along with the idea, that the character is "drunk," rather than observing a few disparate behaviors and objects associated with drunkenness. But so, too,

138 BETWEEN THE LINES

do we passively or actively ignore concrete objects during performance. Sometimes we choose simply to look up at the rafters; other times, we focus our attention on concrete theatrical objects; and other times, we may let our imaginations choose to place more mental energy on concrete theatrical objects than those concrete objects that may break the illusion of theatre.

In these instances, as stated earlier in the book's Introduction, our imaginations do what theatre does, which is what VGA computer monitors of the late 1980s attempted to do: make 256 colors feel, or *cohere* in a manner that felt, as though we are viewing millions or an infinite number of colors, as a means to smooth over the incomplete.[15] So that the playtext coheres when on the stage, theatre requires extratextual *correspondence* to our world. Existing between the lines, these extratextual elements are the blank spaces of theatre that need to be filled in by performance(s), but even more important, filled in by the audiences' imaginations.

Imagined Objects and Spaces: Theatre versus Other Art Forms

Why are the imagined objects and spaces of theatre different, or at least how are they conceptualized and understood differently, than the imagined spaces of other art forms?

Film

There are plenty of times that people miss little details in film, meaning that viewing experiences can be different for different viewers; however, no *extra*visual details are required in viewing a film. In some ways, one could even argue that no extravisual details exist as related to the film, as the film and everything in its frame offer the complete fictional world of the film. Sure, one can

TRUTHFULNESS IN THEATRE 139

go back and view a film multiple times and each time come away with a more complete understanding of the film; however, within the frame of film, we see everything in rich detail. Props do not need imagination to fill in: the concrete object is *there*. And there is nothing else that needs or cannot be shown in the frame, as it is (at least theoretically) the full scene that the director imagines. The frame of film works like a narrator that shows, not tells, us the world that the narrator (or, really, rather, the director) wants us to see.

Literature

Much as in film, the narrator frames the world for us, what he or she wants us to see, and as a reader, we buy into a contractual agreement that this is the narrator's lens through which we view the world. Furthermore, and maybe the most important distinction here among these three art forms, *literature only operates in the imagination*, as besides the reality of the ink on the bound paper, there is no physical existence to a novel or short story. There are plenty of conceptual empty spaces in literature, but the difference with theatre is that there is no material reality to the reading process; however, in theatre, the audience witnesses real bodies, moving through real space, in real time.

Theatre

While lighting and stage design can demarcate and hope to frame the action of the play in such a way as to, sometimes, obfuscate the fact that we sit within feet outside of the world of the play, many plays, however, make no such attempt at hiding the strings of theatre. Furthermore, even on Broadway and the West End, even with almost unlimited budgets, there is a bare-bones reality to even the most elaborate of stagings. Much of this has to do with

140   BETWEEN THE LINES

the fact that in its totality, a performance event is (1) not quite an exact time-place-space-defined event, (2) too complex to observe all aspects of the event, and (3) often based on different subjective understandings of the event based on different subjective experiences of the individual spectators.

Conclusion

Theatri Topia for the Curious

Constants, Variables, and Theatre's Rules of Engagement

Within these *utopias*, *theatri topia* work by their own rules of engagement. Theatre is not a (formal) game, per se, in the same sense that David Z. Saltz has spent a long part of his career developing a wonderful ludic theory of theatre, but theatre's reliance on play and players raises the specter of analogies to games. Games offer a certain set of rules, and the outcome is unknown. We play games because we do not know the outcome. But gambling, similarly, whether based on chance or skill, has an unknown outcome, where one is exposed to loss or gain, and a wager is based upon perceived odds of an outcome coming to pass. According to the *Oxford English Dictionary*, "game" is an etymon of "gamble," "gambler," and "gambling" (*OED*: "gamble," v.).

Constants and Variables in Play

In arguably the first "modern" play, the insufferable repetition of death and despair thematically opens the play *Danton's Death* (1835), by Georg Buchner, with a game of cards. Flirting with a woman at the card table, by "plott[ing] an affair with the queen," Hérault, a deputy of the National Convention, turns the physical action of a card game into a sexual advance: "The kings and queens

---

Between the Lines. Michael Y. Bennett, Oxford University Press. © Oxford University Press 2024.
DOI: 10.1093/9780197691700.003.0009

142 BETWEEN THE LINES

fall on top of each other so indecently and the jacks pop up right after."[1] The stacking of the cards, however, not only mirrors the physical nature of procreation and birth but ominously points out the continual "fall" of kings and queens: the indecent, possibly early or treacherous fall of the kings and queens is followed by the rise of more than one jack, vying for power and the throne. This drama, played out with the flick of the cards, only lasts until the cards are reshuffled, and then the same drama can be played over again. The fall of kings and queens is left, somewhat, to chance. However, "It costs money."[2] And to get into this drama, to participate in this rise and fall requires a price: some win and some lose. But there is always a winner, and there is always a loser. And the cards do not care that previous winners come out losers in the end. The cards have no memory. Each card player, however, is very aware of the object of the game and remembers each win and loss.

In a card game, each time the cards are shuffled, different players play out different hands. However, are all bound by the rules of the game. Apart from issues of performance and even history (both examined above), the idea of a card game needs to be teased out even further. Each deck of cards contains a finite number of cards and a finite number of specific cards. And the rules of a card game determine each card's *value* and *use*. So while every game of cards will have the same rules, and the cards will have the same value and use, there are multiple types of card games. And, therefore, the value and use of each specific card are unstable. For example, in one type of card game, an ace might be the most valuable card (or most useful), while in another it might be a liability. So while a deck of cards may appear to have an independent, logical set of values, this could not be further from the truth. In basic mathematics, the integral numbers 2–10 have a constant value. Humans *use* mathematics and these numbers (which, while they *are* human constructs, they are supposedly universal, more or less logical *concepts* independent of subjectivity). In a game of cards, however, the cards are subject to human will and, maybe more importantly, human desire. And it

CONCLUSION 143

is this human element that destabilizes the value and use of things (i.e., in this case the specific cards)—things that appear to be logical concepts or objects independent of human input—and turns them into things that manifest themselves to us only through subjectivity.

Card games and theatre play out like a reshuffled game of cards with different players and different strategies and slightly different scenarios, but they are bound by the rules of either the card game or the rules of the text: the card game functioning as the perfect analogy for the synchronicity and diachronicity of particulars and the universals. The reliance, then, is on memory to carry the past and that which is forever lost to time forward.

In Suzan-Lori Parks's *Topdog/Underdog*, to return to the play described in the Introduction, the gamble turns into, rather, the hustle: the gambler believes they are gambling; the hustler already knows that the odds are almost exclusively in the hustler's favor. Three-card monte has a more or less predetermined outcome, unlike a shuffled game of cards. In some ways, then, too, the playwright is more like a hustler, in that they know the outcome of the play, and hope that the audience will experience their intended goals (if they have them).

The Logic of Theatre: Ten Rules of Engagement

Theatre has its own rules of engagement that set the limits of what is known and what is unknown[3]:

1. **The Textual Contract**

   If x *were* the case, the playwright and reader/audience *must* agree, that then y *would have been*, or at least *could or might have been*, the case.

   1. If this agreement is not made by the reader/audience, OR

144   BETWEEN THE LINES

2. If the playwright does not write up a counterfactual conditional that demonstrates the minimum probability/possibility of "might" or "could"—if x were the case, then y might/could have been the case—

THEN the reader/audience experiences disbelief and/or displeasure.

2. The Actor's Contract

If x *were* the case, (we [i.e., actor and audience] must agree that) then y *might be* the case.

3. Speeches

If it *were* the case that (character) S *said p*, then (character) T *would have responded* by saying q.

4. Stage Directions

If a is defined as the delivery of (speech) p, then a contains a set of permissible possibilities (i.e., $a_1, a_2, a_3, \ldots$).

If the playwright wants only *one* permissible a, then stage directions r are required, either (1) to limit a to one possible a (e.g., a_2), or (2) a is limited *enough* by r to contain a set of a's that the playwright desires and/or deems permissible.

5. Exposition

The playwright writes an x—that is, and/or [the situation of] x—such that if x-then . . .

In Greek/Roman plays, if x, then y is *the necessary* projection of x.

In Renaissance and after plays, if x, then y is *a possible* projection of x.

6. First Impressions

Sets the x in the (generic) counterfactual conditional, if it were the case that x, then _____.

CONCLUSION 145

7. Believing an Actor

Once x is defined, then the actor's projection of x—if x, then [actor's projection]—(1) must not depart from the projections derived from x, and (2) needs to change mismatched two-past counterfactual to one-past might counterfactual to preserve feeling of "liveness."

8. Conflict

Given b (i.e., the set of factors) and c (i.e., the set of individuals), then given the co-presence of the two sets (i.e., b and c), in (1) Greek/Roman drama, z is the *necessary* (unavoidable) outcome, or in (2) Renaissance drama onward, z is a *possible* outcome.

9. Resolution

Given (conflict) z, the same sets of b factors and c individuals that make z possible/necessary *must also satisfy* the projection toward the resolution, *except* in the case where/when z *changes the set(s)* of b factors and/or c individuals.

10. Between the Lines

If x were the case, then *everything* that possibly follows from x—*except not-x*—is *possible/permissible*.

Ultimately, these ten rules of theatrical engagement suggest that theatre itself promotes curious behaviors, both for people within putting on the play and for the audience viewing the play.

Curiosity and Theatre

Curiosity is integral to the process of coherence and subsumption in the theatre, as curiosity is about inquiring as to what is *not* there.

146 BETWEEN THE LINES

And as this entire book has centered on investigating the empty spaces of theatre, we have spent a lot of time and energy thinking about what is not there. Here, I claim that curiosity is connected with a cluster of different behaviors that all have to do with the gathering and/or confirmation of knowledge (related, in this sense, to what knowledge is not possessed, to what is not there). And as theatre, as discussed especially in Chapter 3, is understood best (I claim) through betting behaviors where one makes a bet as to what will unfold based upon their present knowledge and various degrees of belief, I claim that theatre is an endeavor for the curious and one that promotes curiosity (or, rather, curious behaviors): besides entertainment, this is theatre's value.

In what appears to be the only philosophical monograph devoted to the topic of curiosity, in *The Philosophy of Curiosity*, Ilhan Inan (2012) argues against equating *curiosity* with the *desire to know*. Instead, Inan (2012) claims that curiosity emanates from a self-awareness of one's own ignorance and by possessing the linguistic ability to refer to the unknown (what Inan terms *inostensible reference*). Inan proposes that curious inquiry takes such forms as the *conditional*, "if . . . then," or *disjunctive* questions (2012: 119). As I interpret Inan's claims, Inan's view of curiosity rests on two *innate* abilities that one either possesses or does not possess, or possesses to varying degrees (i.e., self-awareness and linguistic ability). Inan's view appears to describe curious *people*.

I do not think, however, that one needs (or needs to possess the ability) to be (1) self-aware of one's own limits of knowledge or (2) possess knowledge of what one does not know (e.g., Meno's paradox, which forms some the basis of Inan's claims [Inan 2012: 67, 125]). Instead, I claim that one merely needs to be able to (1) describe what is known (to oneself) and (2) ask (at least one form of) two types of questions that reflect two *types* of curiosity (that are not mutually exclusive): a *creative (generative)* type and an *inquisitive (descriptive)* type. Finally, I claim that curiosity refers to

CONCLUSION 147

a *cluster of different behaviors* that are all loosely connected to the creation and/or acquisition of knowledge.

While philosophers, psychologists, and neuroscientists appear to see curiosity as referring to a single *behavior* or a single *drive* (whether the search to know, to understand the unknown, or a general information-seeking drive),[4] I think this—what I see as an incorrect—*conflation* explains why there has remained a certain *je ne sais quoi* air to curiosity. Instead, I claim that curiosity refers to a *cluster of different behaviors* that are *loosely* connected to the acquisition and/or creation of knowledge. I claim that curiosity refers to two main *types* of general inquiry that each have a different function and/or purpose. Further, each of these two types has (at least) two forms that express curiosity. I call these two types creative curiosity (which is generative) and inquisitive curiosity (which is descriptive).

Arguing against the ideas that curiosity derives from (1) self-awareness of one's own knowledge and what one does not know, (2) is a linguistic ability that allows one to refer to the unknown, and (3) is a single drive or behavior, I claim that curiosity describes, rather, a cluster of different types of behaviors that are loosely connected to the creation and/or acquisition of knowledge. The logic behind different types of curious behaviors takes the form of, either, the counterfactual or the counterfactual conditional to generate knowledge, or it takes the form to acquire and/or verify (existing) bodies of knowledge.

One could object and argue that curiosity merely describes a *desire* to ask questions or, even more simply, describes the traits of a person who asks many questions. One could also argue that asking questions is a product of a curious being, or of being curious. I would answer that in some people who display curious behaviors, the above objections may hold true. The issue, however, is whether curiosity describes an internal drive(s) and/or curious people, or whether curiosity describes the behavior of asking curious-type

148   BETWEEN THE LINES

questions. My claim suggests more of the latter; however, it does not discount the former, in that both can hold true.

Creative (generative) curiosity operates through the logic of (1) *counterfactuals* and, furthering Inan's notion of the conditional construction (2012), the logic of creative (generative) curiosity *also* operates through, I claim, (2) *counterfactual conditionals*, with (1) and (2) taking such possible forms:

> [*counterfactual logic*]
>   (1) x is the case, but what *if* not-x *were* the case?
> [*counterfactual conditional logic*]
>   (2) *If* not-x *were* the case, *then* what *would* proceed from not-x?

The logic and function of these two forms of questions or lines of inquiry are to understand and/or create that which is not (currently) present and/or existent. Curiosity of this type refers to having counterfactual propositional attitudes toward objects.

Inquisitive (descriptive) curiosity, however, is concerned with *factual knowledge* (or *belief*, or *justified belief*) and operates through the logic of two separate principles regarding knowledge—(3) *acquisition* and/or (4) *verification*—with (3) and (4) taking such possible forms:

> [*logic of acquisition*]
>   (3) I know (or believe, or are justified in believing) x is the case, but what is the case of not-x?
> [*logic of verification*]
>   (4) Is my knowledge (or belief, or justified belief) of x correct?

The logic and function of these forms of questions or lines of inquiry are concerned with levels of knowledge related to (existing) bodies of knowledge. The first form, (3), related to existing bodies of knowledge (i.e., knowledge acquisition), comes with its own set of possible functions and desires (that may or may not overlap in any given line of inquiry): (1) the novelty/excitement of encountering something new; (2) the reward of expertise (whether internally or externally motivated); and (3) the avoidance of ignorance (whether internally or externally motivated).

Further, my claim, thus far, could be argued to have its flaws, for it only describes *intellectually* curious questions. Thinking about the limits of my own claim, is in not possible that someone can be sensorially curious, or, rather, display different types of curious behaviors around the senses? Just as psychologists are in wide agreement now about theories of multiple intelligences, doesn't an adventurous eater or an extreme athlete (who pushes one's body to its extreme limits) display curious behaviors, too?

Despite the objections raised, and that curiosity has mostly been seen as a mental process or drive by philosophers, psychologists, and neuroscientists, I think that the logic of questions that take the form of the *counterfactual* or *counterfactual conditional* to generate knowledge or take the form to *acquire* or *verify* existing bodies of knowledge also pertains to *sensory* behaviors. In seeking to broaden the conception of curiosity, I am not suggesting that everyone is equally curious, or displays different types of curious behaviors in different ways in, though differing, equal amounts, but only that curiosity describes a cluster of different types of different behaviors. While I do not claim, again, that everyone is equally curious, these claims hope to shed light on the logic behind different curious behaviors.

As such, just as one may teach the logic behind the illogical nature of fallacies to help improve thinking logically, it is my hope that one may also teach the logic behind different types of curious behaviors to help improve behaving curiously. Theatre, with its own rules of engagement, might just be one way to teach and develop curious behaviors, a cluster of behaviors sorely needed in this so-called post-truth moment in history.

Glossary of Terms and Concepts

Abstract object An "abstract object" is *immaterial*; it may, or may not, exist.

Coherence (coherence theory of truth) The truth of a statement or a belief can only be judged in terms of how well it coheres with other held statements or beliefs, and as such, truth is thought of as degrees of truth.

Concrete object A "concrete object," and a "concrete action," have a *material* reality.

Correspondence (correspondence theory of truth) The correspondence theory of truth holds that something is true if it corresponds with a fact and/or a state of affairs.

Degrees of belief Also known as *credences*, a degree of belief is how strongly a particular belief is held to be true.

Experiences

 Individual (experience) An "individual experience" is one's *own experience* of an action/object.

 Private (experience) A "private experience" is a *singular and unique experience* an individual has to an action/object.

 Public (experience) A "public experience" is when *two or more people experience the same action/object*.

 Shared (experience) A "shared experience" is *when two or more individuals have the same individual experience* when experiencing the same action/object.

Extrinsic properties Extrinsic properties are all the properties of an object that are not intrinsic properties.

152　GLOSSARY OF TERMS AND CONCEPTS

Intrinsic properties Via David Friedell, via David Lewis, "A thing has its intrinsic properties in virtue of the way that thing itself, and nothing else, is."

Parallax When viewing (broadly defined) a concrete object or action (broadly defined), "parallax" is the (inherent) resultant error that is due to one's *perspective* (broadly defined).

Performance "Performance" refers to *the entirety of an artistic idea and its material enactment(s)*. "Performance," then, subsumes "theatre" as a broader term. That is, traditionally, "theatre" refers to the combination of a dramatic text and the performance of a dramatic text; "performance" is broader in that it still holds the category of "theatre" within but also works for the category of non-text-based performance. Further, using this idea that performance refers to the entirety of an artistic idea and its material enactment(s), performance casts a broader net, here subsuming other art forms like film and television (as well as more traditional "performing arts" like dance, opera, music, etc.).

Performance event A "performance event" is a specific and singular enactment of a performance. "Performance events" are specific instances of a performance, often localized and restricted to a specific time and space/place.

Performance text A "performance text" refers to a written text that sets the rules and/or guidelines for a performance event. Note: Not all "performances" have a "performance text."

Properties (in the theatre)

Distinct properties Distinct properties are found explicitly in the dramatic text and are necessarily *true*.

Subsumed properties *Subsumed properties* are derived from the distinct properties that are explicit in the dramatic text, and these properties, which can be true, are derived properties (i.e., derived by entailment, other generic facts, and/or interpretation and/or triangulation).

GLOSSARY OF TERMS AND CONCEPTS   153

Truthful properties *Truthful properties* are a type of subsumed properties that may or may not be *truly* applied to a character (i.e., they may even be *falsely* applied to a character) and may not be derived from any of these ways, but yet these subsumed properties speak to something *truthful* about theatrical characters and/or theatrical worlds. A truthful property contains at least one truth, even if the overall state of that object is false. These properties may be thought of as *truthful suggestions*. They are derived by relations in the text that are weaker than entailment, namely *textual assertions that do not necessarily fit the actual world* or by *truthful suggestions* that are not implied by any of the aforementioned ways, but yet simply *make sense*, if you will, or *can* make sense.

Proposition A semi-technical term that has broad and different usage in philosophy; here, I will be using it to refer to the thought content of a statement that can be true or false.

Re-creation (re-created object) *Re-creation* describes both the process and the abstract object that comes into being through a recombination and/or unique cluster of actually existing, concrete and/or abstract objects, where we can call the resultant object a *re-created object*.

Re-positioning (re-positioned object) *Re-positioning* describes the process by which actually existing objects are viewed/presented in a manner that explore novel relations among its constituent parts. The resultant object that is viewed/presented is a *re-positioned object*.

Superimpose To "superimpose" is to layer and overlap beliefs, justified beliefs, justified true beliefs, and knowledge from numerous individual perspectives to create a more accurate objective understanding of a concrete object or action (broadly defined). "Superimposition" lessens the parallax (i.e., the error caused by observing/experiencing an object from a unique perspective).

154 GLOSSARY OF TERMS AND CONCEPTS

Transworld identity Transworld identity is the nature of identity across possible worlds. For something to have transworld identity means it has the same identity across all possible worlds.

Triangulate In the most literal sense, "triangulating" describes the process of the superimposition of beliefs, justified beliefs, and knowledge about an object in situations where *three* minds are all experiencing the same object. More broadly, "triangulation" simply means superimposing the experiences of *more than two* minds.

Truth Truth is the state of something being true (versus being false).

Truthfulness Truthfulness is the state of something containing at least one truth, even if the overall state of something is false.

Viewer(s) A "viewer" is an individual who attends (or attended) a performance event. "Viewers" refers to a group of individuals (i.e., $viewer_1$ + $viewer_2$ + $viewer_3$, etc.), all of whom attend a particular performance event. The focus here in not on viewing, specifically, as a visual process, but as the *mental contemplation* (of an object).

Notes

Introduction

1. Suzan-Lori Parks, *Topdog/Underdog* (New York: Theatre Communications Group, 2001), 3.
2. See Kendall Walton, "Categories of Art," *The Philosophical Review* 79, no. 3 (1970): 334–367. Further, for a retrospective on this article, see "Symposium: 'Categories of Art' at 50" in *Journal of Aesthetics and Art Criticism* 78, no. 1 (Winter 2020): 65–84.
3. W. B. Worthen, *Drama: Between Poetry and Performance* (Malden, MA: Wiley-Blackwell, 2010), xvi.

Chapter 1

1. I am wording it as such, "based on," so as to try to sidestep the issue, here, of the debated relationship between dramatic text and theatrical performance. This phrasing intentionally is somewhat ambiguous and allows for much leeway when it comes to how one conceives the relationship between the dramatic text and the theatrical performance. See Carroll (2001), Saltz (2001), and Hamilton (2001, 2007). I also address this in Bennett (2017), suggesting that both the dramatic text and the theatrical are both "re-creations."
2. One major debate over liveness in theatre and performance studies is over the primacy of theatre being live (or in the *here and now*) and, related to this, whether theatre can be video recorded. For more on this debate, see Peggy Phelan (1993), Philip Auslander's *Liveness* (1997), Elin Diamond's *Unmaking Mimesis* (1997), and, most recently, Daniel Sack's *After Live* (2015).
3. See Hamilton's great description of the ingredients model (2007: 31–33).
4. James R. Hamilton's 2009 article, "The Text-Performance Relation in Theater," in *Philosophy Compass*, captured this debate, a debate that

156 NOTES

with hindsight, really established "philosophy of theatre" as a unique *philosophy of* . . . . Hamilton's essay looks back to the special section in the *Journal of Aesthetics and Art Criticism* (2001), where Noël Carroll, James R. Hamilton, and David Z. Saltz debate about whether theatrical performance is its own art form or a once-removed interpretation of the dramatic text, and then tracks the debate through the majority of that decade.

5. Irit Degani-Raz, "Possible Worlds and the Concept of 'Reference' in the Semiotics of Theater," *Semiotica* 147, no. 1/4 (2003): 307–329; Irit Degani-Raz, "Theatrical Fictional Worlds, Counterfactuals, and Scientific Thought Experiments," *Semiotica* 157, no. 1/4 (2005): 353–375.

Chapter 2

1. Berto, "Modal Meinongianism and Fiction: The Best of Three Worlds," *Philosophical Studies* 152 (2011): 316–321.

2. For some recent articles that either share, take issue with, or offer variations of these three general categories, see Peter Alward, "Description, Disagreement, and Fictional Names," *Canadian Journal of Philosophy* 41, no. 3 (September 2011): 423–448; David Braun, "Empty Names, Fictional Names, Mythical Names," *Nous* 39, no. 4 (2005): 596–631; Iris Einheuser, "Some Remarks on 'Language-Created Entities,'" *Acta Analytica* 24 (2008): 185–192; Anthony Everett, "Pretense, Existence, and Fictional Objects," *Philosophy and Phenomenological Research* 74, no. 1 (January 2007): 56–80; Neil Feit, "Naming and Nonexistence," *The Southern Journal of Philosophy* 47 (2009): 239–262; John Gibson, "Interpreting Words, Interpreting Worlds," *The Journal of Aesthetics and Art Criticism* 64, no. 4 (Fall 2006): 439–450; David Liggins, "Modal Fictionalism and Possible-Worlds Discourse," *Philosophical Studies* 138 (2008): 151–160; Eleonora Orlando, "Fictional Names without Fictional Objects," *Crítica* 40, no. 120 (December 2008): 111–127; Diane Proudfoot, "Possible Worlds Semantics and Fiction," *Journal of Philosophical Logic* 35 (2006): 9–40; Fiora Salis, "Fictional Reports: A Study on the Semantics of Fictional Names," *Theoria* 68 (2010): 175–185; Andrea Sauchelli, "Fictional Objects, Non-Existence, and the Principle of Characterization," *Philosophical Studies* 159 (2012): 139–146; Mark Textor, "Sense-Only-Signs: Frege on Fictional Proper Names," *Grazer Philosophische Studien* 82 (2011): 375–400; and Richard

Woodward, "Is Modal Fictionalism Artificial?" *Pacific Philosophical Quarterly* 92 (2011): 535–560.

3. For more on Meinongian theories, see Berto (2011); D. Jaquette, *Meinongian Logic: The Semantics of Existence and Nonexistence* (Berlin: De Gruyter, 1996); T. Parsons, *Nonexistent Objects* (New Haven, CT: Yale University Press, 1980); G. Priest, *Towards Non-Being: The Logic and Metaphysics of Intentionality* (Oxford: Oxford University Press, 2005); and R. Routley, *Exploring Meinong's Jungle and Beyond* (Canberra: Australian National University, 1980).

4. For more on Fictionalism, see Stuart Brock, "Fictionalism about Fictional Characters," *Nous* 36, no. 1 (2002): 1–21; Gregory Currie, *The Nature of Fiction* (Cambridge: Cambridge University Press, 1990); Gideon Rosen, "Modal Fictionalism," *Mind* 99, no. 395 (July 1990): 327–354; and Kendall Walton, *Mimesis as Make-Believe* (Cambridge, MA: Harvard University Press, 1990).

5. While on a different subject matter and used in a different sense, recognition and re-creation are essential parts of the hermeneutic process for Hans-Georg Gadamer in *Truth and Method* (1960). Gadamer suggests that in interpretation, the person doing the interpretation should not re-create the author's intent. Instead, one should re-cognize one's own interpretation, in that the meaning should be cognized in oneself. Here, I am using the concept of *re-creation* in an entirely different sense than Gadamer.

    Neal Curtis, in arguing that Being is *in medio*, suggests that being-in-the-world is a question of mediation, in that (1) "humans exist in and through language; that this representational technique is our world" (70); (2) "being-in-the world is always being-with-others" (70); and (3) "a sense of self comes *from* a sense *for* the world" (Neal Curtis, "The Human, *In Medio*," *Angelaki* 15, no. 2 [2010]: 70). Curtis concludes that "because our world is created through the technique of representation, the world can always be *re*-presented" (Curtis 2010: 70). Jerry Fodor's notion that mental states are relations between individuals and metal representations also bears mention (see Fodor, "Propositional Attitudes" *The Monist* 61, no. 4 [1978]: 501–523). It is through language (a technique of representation) that the playwright operates. Curtis's thesis, importantly, brings up questions of "representation," which is a topic that has received ample attention as it relates to art and aesthetics. Nelson Goodman's *Languages of Art* (1968), Richard Wollheim's *Art and Its Objects* (1968), and Kendall L. Walton's *Mimesis as Make-Believe* (1990) are books in philosophical

158 NOTES

aesthetics that make foundational arguments about the centrality of representation in understanding art. While there is a slight connotation of *representation* in my idea of "re-creation"—again, to be clear—I am not arguing that theatre is a representation.

What do I mean by "re-creation"? Starting first with just the idea of "creation" (and from there we can understand how re-creation differs from creation), the definition of "creation" (and all of these following definitions come from the *OED*) is simply, "1. a. Something created by divine or natural agency." A slightly more specific definition of "creation," especially as it pertains to connotations of creating art, is, "1. b. An original production of human intelligence, power, skill, or art; *esp.* a work of imagination." Breaking down this latter definition further to understand the constituent parts, the way that "original" appears to be used in the definition of creation is "5. a. Created, composed, or done by a person directly; produced first-hand; not imitated or copied from another." And "Imagination" appeared to be used as "1. a. The power or capacity to form internal images or ideas of objects and situations not actually present to the senses, including remembered objects and situations, and those constructed by mentally combining or projecting images of previously experienced qualities, objects, and situations." Furthermore, this idea that the "internal images or ideas of objects" that are produced by imagination are "not actually present to the senses" is in line with the second definition of "creation": "2. a. The action or process of bringing something into existence from nothing by divine or natural agency; the fact of being so created." Therefore, "creation" has the sense of actualizing *ex nihilo* something "original" (i.e., not present to the senses).

Re-creation, then, is a "re"-production of an "original" "creation." Therefore, what is re-created is not something wholly "created by divine or natural agency," as the prefix "re-" connotes "the general sense of 'back' or 'again'" and denotes "that the action itself is performed a second time." The prefix "re-" should indicate that there is nothing "original" in the final product. Reproduction, replication, and (by extension) duplication all connote something done and/or produced *again*; these are once-removed objects that copy, or are copies of, an original object. However, as a re-"creation," where "re-" is modifying "creation," there is still a sense that what is being created is "not actually present to the senses." In re-creation there exists a residue of creation. Re-creation finds something "that which is left" from creation. Given that re-creation is once removed from creation, re-creation *re*-presents something "created by divine or natural agency."

NOTES 159

Thus, re-creation simultaneously portrays both the world as "created by divine or natural agency" and also *a* world "not actually present to the senses."

6. I am thinking here of Angelika Kratzer's original positions on "lumps of thought," or more specifically and more recently, Kratzer's stance on the relationship between counterfact and fact in Angelika Kratzer, "Facts: Particulars or Information Units?" *Linguistics and Philosophy* 25 (2002): 669.

7. What I do not address is how or why a particular concept is selected or not selected, as this is well beyond the scope of this chapter (and book). I will leave this line of inquiry to more qualified thinkers: philosophers of mind and those in the fields of psychology and the neurosciences. Communication, then, is successful when there exists enough of an overlap and/or convergence in language created by the speaker and interpreted by the receiver of that utterance; if there is not enough of an overlap and/or convergence, then the possibilities for miscommunication arise.

The idea that language, given its inherent level of ambiguity/vagueness, essentially functions via interpretation is probably not much of a revelation. However, my explanation of *interpretation*—through which I claim that language is communicated and understood, brings together discussions of (1) *reference*; (2) *metaphor* (see Israel Scheffler, *Symbolic Worlds: Art, Science, Language, Ritual* [Cambridge: Cambridge University Press, 1997], 74–94. Here, Scheffler provides a wonderful overview of the debates surrounding metaphor. His explanation and critique of Nelson Goodman's contextualist theses and extensional theories of metaphor is extremely in-depth. Scheffler rebuttal of Josef Stern's dismissal of extensional theories of metaphor (because, as Stern argues, substituting co-extensive terms does not always yield the same truth), provides a solid in-road to the debate [Scheffler 1997: 89–94]. My thesis relies on principles of both extension and intension, but is bound to neither of the two in any strict manner); (3) ambiguity/vagueness (for a very good overview of the epistemic problems posed by "vagueness," see Christopher D. Kyle, "Epistemicism and the Problem of Arbitrariness for Vagueness," *Dialogue* [October 2012]. While not commenting directly the concerns of the present book, Andrea Iacona writes persuasively about validity in natural language by examining paradigmatic arguments of vagueness, ambiguity, and context sensitivity: see Andrea Iacona, "Validity and Interpretation," *Australasian Journal of Philosophy* 88, no. 2 [June 2010]:

160　NOTES

247–264); (4) theories of concepts (while my theory of meaning does not deal with the *structure* of concepts, it clearly comments indirectly on the *classical theory of concepts* and *conceptual pluralism*); and brings together (5) propositional semantic theories of meaning (see, particularly, Alfred Tarski, *Introduction to Logic and to the Method of Deductive Sciences*, 2nd ed. [New York: Oxford University Press, 1946]) with (6) nonmentalist theories of meaning (see, particularly, Paul Horwich, *Meaning* [Oxford: Oxford University Press, 1998]).

8. My claim holds that a combinatorial view of fictional referents is not only analogous to a combinatorial view of possible worlds but claims that possible worlds are, themselves, one type of abstract object that I call re-creations. Possible worlds are simply the most complex type of re-creations. This claim, then, interprets possible worlds as an abstract object in realist terms, versus having an ontological status that occupies a third category that lies between realism and fictionalism. It is plausible, then, that my thesis can be interpreted as a type of *ersatz modal realism*; to this interpretation of my claim, I would not be able to fully disagree.

Clearly, my claim of combination and re-combination and re-arrangement is similar to D. M. Armstrong's combinatorial theory (1989). However, I do fall into a fundamentally different camp concerning the ontology and ontological status of possible worlds: I, ultimately, am a *realist* (contra *fictionalists*) in the sense that I claim possible worlds are *abstract objects*, which contrasts with Armstrong's belief that possible worlds occupy an ontological status between realism and fictionalism. Of course, too, Armstrong is describing the ontology of possible worlds, and I start with the ontology of words, and then in *Analytic Philosophy and the World of the Play* build and develop a theory of possible worlds out of the model of the ontology and ontological status of the referent of a word (except proper names with a rigid designation).

Further, these types of *abstract objects* may seemingly be read through the general theoretical umbrella of "combinatorial constructs," a put forth by W. V. O. Quine (1968) and M. J. Cresswell (1973). Combinatorial constructs are made out of a basic "atom," in a sense, that are rearranged via a set-theoretical principles. While William Lycan calls "atoms . . . the fundamental building blocks of our own world" (1978: 305), I am not, however, suggesting that the building blocks of possible worlds are these "atoms." Again, I am suggesting, rather, *concrete objects* and *concrete actions*, instead, are the building blocks of re-creations. While I use "clusters," my assertion does not fall under the umbrella idea that a name refers to a "cluster" or family of descriptions and/or resemblances, most notably as put forth by Wittgenstein (1953: §79) and, more specifically, by Searle (1958). Because I build up a hierarchy from referents associated with the parts of words, it might seem to appear that I advocate for some type of *linguistic entity* as the building block of a theory about possible worlds, a theory Bricker (1987) persuasively argues against. For the sake of clarity, I am not arguing that linguistic entities are the building blocks of possible worlds.

9. Re-positioned objects in other art forms:

   Music re-positions *intervals* of time and notes/sounds.

   Literature re-positions *words* in sentences/lines.

   Dance re-positions *space and bodies* across time.

   Architecture and sculpture re-position *shapes* in three dimensions.

   Painting and drawing re-position *lines*, *shapes*, and *colors* in two dimensions.

   Photography re-positions to *object(s)*.

10. I make this claim, in part, because in Hills (2017)—the article entry on "Metaphor" in the *Stanford Encyclopedia of Philosophy*—not only starts and prefaces the entire article with I. A. Richards's tenor and vehicle/subject, but essentially every section of the article refers in one way or another to these terms, either directly or indirectly.

11. For a complete breakdown of all the literary forms that are encompassed by *meshalim*, see Jeremy Schipper, *Parables and Conflict in the Hebrew Bible* (Cambridge: Cambridge University Press, 2009).

12. Dodd (1965) is discussing, specifically, *parables* in this passage, but the basic thesis of the entire book is that Dodd defines parables as metaphors.

13. For much more on *brute force accounts* of metaphor, as well as *pragmatic twist accounts* of metaphor, see Hills (2017).

14. Husserl, Anscombe, Ayer, and Dennett are lurking in the background for their work on *intentionality*, as are—even more so—ordinary language philosophers such as Searle, Strawson, Grice, and Austin. For more, specifically, on the study of intention as it relates to the theatre, see David Z. Saltz, "The Reality of Doing: Real Speech Acts in the Theatre," *Method Acting Reconsidered: Theory, Practice, Future*, ed. David Krasner (New York: St. Martin's, 2000), 61–79; and Michael Goldman, "'Hamlet': Entering the Text," *Theatre Journal* 44, no. 4 (December 1992): 449–460. Though not specifically concerning intentionality, the idea is inherent in the study of theatre semiotics, which was most prominent in theatre/drama studies in the 1980s and early 1990s. See Elaine Aston and George Savona, *Theatre as*

162 NOTES

Sign System: A Semiotics of Text and Performance; Marvin Carlson, *Theatre Semiotics: Signs of Life*; Keir Elam, *The Semiotics of Theatre and Drama*; Erika Fischer-Lichte, *The Semiotics of Theater*; Marco de Marinis, *The Semiotics of Performance*; and Patrice Pavis, *Languages of the Stage: Essays in the Semiology of Theatre*.

Chapter 3

1. While the literature on the "Gettier Problem," responses to the "Gettier Problem," and the literature on justified beliefs is exhaustive, I am less interested in dealing (directly) with the "Gettier Problem" than using it both to introduce some central concerns in contemporary epistemology and to use it to get to some problems inherent in the epistemic study of other minds. This idea of justified belief is important because it straddles the two poles of what we believe and of what we know. What we often assume is our knowledge of a performance is, instead, largely, our justified beliefs about a performance. Most likely, we could arguably agree that one can have knowledge of, say, the words spoken by an actor X or who is playing character Y.

   For more on the literature on justified beliefs, see the following as a starting place: R. M. Chisholm, *Theory of Knowledge* (Englewood Cliffs, NJ: Prentice Hall, 1966/1977/1989); R. Feldman, "An Alleged Defect in Gettier Counterexamples," *Australasian Journal of Philosophy* 52 (1974): 68–69; S. Hetherington, *Knowledge Puzzles: An Introduction to Epistemology* (Boulder, CO: Westview Press, 1996); S. Hetherington, *Good Knowledge, Bad Knowledge: On Two Dogmas of Epistemology* (Oxford: Oxford University Press, 2001); R. Keefe and P. Smith, eds., *Vagueness: A Reader* (Cambridge, MA: The MIT Press, 1996); K. Lehrer, "Knowledge, Truth and Evidence," *Analysis* 25 (1965): 168–175; K. Lehrer, "Why Not Scepticism?" *The Philosophical Forum* 2 (1971): 283–298; D. Lewis, "Elusive Knowledge," *Australasian Journal of Philosophy* 74 (1996): 549–567; W. G. Lycan, "Evidence One Does Not Possess," *Australasian Journal of Philosophy* 55 (1977): 114–126; W. G. Lycan, "On the Gettier Problem Problem," *Epistemology Futures*, ed. S. Hetherington (Oxford: Oxford University Press, 2006); P. K. Moser, ed., *Empirical Knowledge: Readings in Contemporary Epistemology* (Totowa, NJ: Rowman & Littlefield, 1986); G. S. Pappas and M. Swain, eds., *Essays*

NOTES 163

on *Knowledge and Justification* (Ithaca, NY: Cornell University Press, 1978); M. D. Roth and L. Galis, eds., *Knowing: Essays in the Analysis of Knowledge* (New York: Random House, 1970); R. K. Shope, *The Analysis of Knowing: A Decade of Research* (Princeton, NJ: Princeton University Press, 1983); and T. Williamson, *Knowledge and Its Limits* (Oxford: Oxford University Press, 2000).

2. For more on the connection among belief, experience, and accuracy, see Susanna Siegel, "The Contents of Perception" (2016), *The Stanford Encyclopedia of Philosophy*, ed. Edward N. Zalta, https://plato.stanford.edu/entries/perception-contents. In particular, see section 2.2, "Beliefs and Experiences":

> There are many ways of developing the idea that experiences are assessable for accuracy. One idea is that the contents of experience derive in some fashion from the contents of beliefs, so that experiences bear some constitutive link to beliefs. Three sorts of constitutive links to belief have been discussed in the literature. The first is that experiences are *acquisitions* of beliefs; the second is that they are *dispositions* to form beliefs; the third is that they are *grounds* of dispositions to form beliefs. A fourth position simply identifies experiences with beliefs about how things look (Gluer 2009), or even more simply, with beliefs whose content characterizes the way things look (Bryne 2016).

3. See Bennett, *World of the Play*, 64–67; also indirectly discussed in Michael Y. Bennett, "Intrinsic-Extrinsic Properties in Theatre," *Philosophy and Literature* 45, no. 1 (2021): 34–38.

4. Stephan Hartmann and Jan Sprenger, "Bayesian Epistemology," *Routledge Companion to Epistemology* (London: Routledge, 2010), 610. For a more technical account of the claims of, and arguments against, Bayesian epistemology, see Alan Hájek and Stephan Hartmann, "Bayesian Epistemology," *A Companion to Epistemology*, ed. J. Dancy et al. (Oxford: Blackwell, 2010), 94–106.

5. There is a vast and ever-expanding field of literature on Bayesian epistemology. As a great starting place for further study, see Jürgen Landes, "Bayesian Epistemology," *Oxford Bibliographies* (2021), https://www.oxfordbibliographies.com/display/document/obo-9780195396577/obo-9780195396577-0417.xml. For a systematic (and magisterial) introduction to the latest trends in the field, see Michael G. Titelbaum, *Fundamentals of Bayesian Epistemology*, vols. I and II (Oxford: Oxford University Press, 2022). For a more technical account and overview of Bayesian epistemology, see William Talbott, "Bayesian Epistemology," *The*

164 NOTES

Stanford Encyclopedia of Philosophy (Winter 2016 edition), ed. Edward N. Zalta, https://plato.stanford.edu/archives/win2016/entries/epistemology-bayesian/.

Bayesian epistemology is a subfield within the wider field of Bayesianism, which spans many fields within philosophy, as well as statistics (most naturally) and psychology. For an introduction to the broader field of Bayesianism, see Kenny Easwaran, "Bayesianism," *Oxford Bibliographies* (2022), https://www.oxfordbibliographies.com/display/document/obo-9780195396577/obo-9780195396577-0204.xml.

6. Hartmann and Sprenger, "Bayesian Epistemology," 609. See also Talbott, "Bayesian Epistemology," particularly, section "2. A Simple Principle of Conditionalization."

7. *Modals* express possibility, permissibility, or necessity. Modals are *qualifiers* that express permissibility or the likelihood of something coming to pass or being true. Examples of modality in the English language include modal verbs/modal auxiliaries (such as *would, could, might, will, can, may,* etc.) and other expressions of modality (such as *ought to, it is possible that, perhaps, maybe,* etc.). Let us examine the expectations that playwrights have, or said in another way, the expectations that are set up in the text by way of the counterfactual and modals:

> If x *were* the case, the playwright and reader/audience *must* agree, that then y *would have been,* or at least, *could* or *might have been,* the case.*

[*NOTE: *If this agreement is not made by the reader/audience, or, if the playwright does not write a counterfactual conditional that demonstrates the minimum probability/possibility of "might" or "could"—i.e., if x were the case, then y might/could have been the case—then the reader/audience experiences disbelief and/or displeasure.*]

8. Donald Davidson, *Subjective, Intersubjective, Objective* (Oxford: Oxford University Press, 2001), 128.

9. Davidson, *Subjective, Intersubjective, Objective,* 88. For more on Davidson, and an explanation of his triangular externalism, see M. Cristina Amoretti and Gerhard Preyer, "Introduction: Mind, Knowledge, and Communication in Triangular Externalism," *Triangulation: From an Epistemological Point of View,* ed. M. Cristina Amoretti and Gerhard Preyer (Boulder, CO: Ontos, 2011), 15–19.

10. My account of triangular knowledge from the perspective of the philosophy of mind, largely, takes an externalist point of view, where mental content is individuated by the outside world, or "the content of the

NOTES 165

mental states depends upon or is individuated by external objects and events" (Amoretti and Preyer," Introduction: Mind, Knowledge, and Communication in Triangular Externalism," 11).

11. Hájek and Hartmann, "Bayesian Epistemology," 101 and 102. For more on Bayesian confirmation theory, see Talbott, "Bayesian Epistemology," particularly, section, "4. Bayesian Confirmation Theory."

12. The epistemic problem presented by Gettier's two examples has come to be known as the "Gettier Problem." For the sake of brevity, here is just Gettier's first case. Smith and Jones both applied for the same job, but Smith has strong evidence that "(d) Jones is the man who will get the job, and Jones has ten coins in his pocket" because the evidence gathered by Smith might be that the president of the company said that Jones would get the job and Smith had, ten minutes prior, counted ten coins in Jones's pocket. Proposition (d) entails that "(e) The man who will get the job has ten coins in his pocket," which Smith accepts on the grounds of (d), for which Smith has strong evidence. As Gettier says, "Smith is clearly justified in believing that (e) is true." However, Gettier continues his thought experiment: What if, unknown to Smith, he (i.e., Smith) gets the job and not Jones? And what if, it is also the case, that Smith also has ten coins in his own pocket? It turns out, as Gettier explains, that (1) (e) is true, (2) Smith believes that (e) is true, and (3) Smith is justified in believing that (e) is true. However, while (e) *is* true, this is the all-important point: Smith does not *know* that (e) is true (Gettier 1963: 122). In short, Smith has a *justified belief* and that justified belief turns out to be *true*, yielding a *justified true belief*. However, Smith does *not* have *knowledge* of the truth of the situation. The "Gettier Problem," thus, exposes some of the differences between truth and knowledge.

13. I am not arguing for a *semantic* contextualism put forth, generally, in "Epistemic Contextualism" (EC). Given that this is *not* what this book is concerned with, I will simply point the reader in the direction of an excellent introduction on the subject: "Epistemic Contextualism" in *Stanford Encyclopedia of Philosophy*.

14. Of course, directors, too, quite often make changes to the dramatic text (or, after, the script that they use for performance). Most often these changes are small deletions of lines here and there, but sometimes there are additions, substantial deletions, or alterations. For more on changes made to artworks and who can, or cannot, make these changes, see David Friedell, "Why Can't I Change Bruckner's *Eighth Symphony*?" *Philosophical Studies* 177 (2020): 805–882.

166 NOTES

15. This is the grand joke of Jorge Luis Borges's short story "Pierre Menard, Author of the Quixote" and also provides the philosophical backbone behind Borges's short story "The Library of Babel."

16. For a playful (or theatrical) take on *qualia*, see Eric Lormand, "*Qualia!* (Now Showing at a Theater Near You)," *Philosophical Topics* 22 (1994): 127–156.

Chapter 4

1. While the majority of Bennett (2017) develops its thesis of "re-creation" alongside the possible worlds thesis, Chapter 5 thinks about both *local* and *global* approaches when evaluating theatrical characters across possible worlds. That is, the majority of Bennett (2017) takes a global approach to the possible worlds thesis, while Chapter 5 contemplates some problems posed by a local approach to possible worlds, much in the vein of situation semantics.

2. See also Kratzer (2019), particularly § 7 on minimality and exemplification, as these are two ideas related to subsumption and distinctness.

3. Bennett *Problems . . .* But yet "a 'witness' tells/recalls the story as they see/ saw it; thus, directors, actors, and designers (not necessarily intentionally, but inevitably) create narratorial bias through which each actor-character-witness is playing out their own side—the character's own personal viewpoint of what transpired—of the story as is "presently performed" (e.g., think of the narratorial bias that the other character accuse The Father of in Luigi Pirandello's *Six Characters in Search of an Author*)." Bennett *Problems . . .*

Chapter 5

1. Fabio Pianesi and Achille C. Varzi suggest that the field of events can be broken down into the following general groups of focus: events as universals; events as particulars; the indeterminacy and vagueness of speaking about events; the logical form of names of and propositions about events; that the semantics of events could be extended to discuss

NOTES 167

states; and linguistic applications regarding events (*Speaking of Events*, Fabio Pianesi et al., eds. [Oxford: Oxford University Press, 2000]), 3–47.

2. Michael Y. Bennett, *Analytic Philosophy and the World of the Play* (London: Routledge, 2017), 63–64. These observations are made in a larger conversation referencing "Leibniz's Law" where a theatrical performance must necessarily, because of the change in medium, be different than the dramatic text, and thus, performance is not merely a reproduction of an original.

3. D. Wilson (2011), "Relevance and the Interpretation of Literary Works," UCL Working Papers in Linguistics 23: 69–80, http://www.ucl.ac.uk/psychlangsci/research/linguistics/publications/uclwpl23, at p. 77. See also K. Bach (2003) "Speech Acts," in *Routledge Encyclopedia of Philosophy* (London: Routledge).

4. M. Brand, "Particulars, Events, and Actions," in *Action Theory: Proceedings of the Winnipeg Conference on Human Action*, ed. M. Brand and D. Walton (Dordrecht: Reidel, 1976), 133–158.

5. Susan L. Feagin, personal email, December 20, 2022.

6. One prominent scholarly conversation in theatre studies in the 2000s was the examination of the dual notions of "theatricality" and "anti-theatricality," the two of which investigate the changing ideas about how "theatrical" was used and conceived throughout history, as sometimes (among many other things) "theatrical" had at times and places a nonmimetic connotation and at other times and places a mimetic connotation. For extensive investigations into both words, see Tracy C. Davis and Thomas Postlewait, eds., *Theatricality* (Cambridge: Cambridge University Press, 2004); Alan Ackerman and Martin Puchner, eds., *Against Theatre: Creative Destructions on the Modernist Stage* (New York: Palgrave Macmillan, 2006).

7. Daniel Sack's previously mentioned 2015 book, *After Live*, is centrally based upon the notion that performance is guided by the idea of "possibility," and Sack's thesis is intended to speak to the "liveness" debate:

> Since performance is always happening now, these concepts speak of a present moment's outlook toward the future not as a relation with a divorced entity, wherein the future might represent a remote island of time, but as an extension of what is immediately before us. These futures belong to the present. . . . *Possibility* projects into the future an event or entity that resembles an already known actuality, a future designated by the terms and conventions of the past and used in the present. (6)

168 NOTES

While the idea presented here in this chapter is clearly related to Sack's book and our conclusions are similar, I am approaching these ideas of "possibility" and "potentiality" from two different angles: (1) the perspective of abductive logic in relation to both modal and formal logic, and (2) by extending and building off of the thesis of my earlier 2012 book, *Narrating the Past through Theatre*:

> Through the performance process, the past, both in its limitation to a strict time and place and in its timelessness, repeats for its current and its future (not-yet-existent) audiences. . . . Although it is the performance/production of the modern history play that both allows the past to meet the present and gives the past the ability to be translated to future audiences, it is the modern playwright who, when he or she finishes penning a history play, has instantaneously fused the past with the future. For the text (in this specific case, hailing the past) needs the potential of production to consummate itself. Each performance brings the past to the present, but the text inherently contains the possibilities of future stagings. . . . Ultimately, [modern history plays] bring the past, present, and future together in the tense of *always*. (9–10)

8. Peggy Phelan, *Unmarked: The Politics of Performance* (London: Routledge, 1993), 194.
9. Erika Fischer-Lichte, *The Transformative Power of Performance: A New Aesthetics*, trans. Saskya Iris Jain (London: Routledge, 2008), 94.
10. Fischer-Lichte, *The Transformative Power of Performance*, 94.
11. Fischer-Lichte, *The Transformative Power of Performance*, 73 and 94.
12. A. A. Rini and M. J. Cresswell, *The World-Time Parallel* (Cambridge: Cambridge University Press, 2012), 16–17.
13. In a novel, a *narrator* is *actively telling* the reader a story that is either in the past, present, or future.
14. Michael Y. Bennett, *Narrating the Past Through Theatre: Four Crucial Texts* (New York: Palgrave Macmillan, 2012).
15. Carlota S. Smith, "Tense and Temporal Interpretation," *Lingua* 117 (2007): 421.
16. Michela Ippolito, "Semantic Composition and Presupposition Projection in Subjunctive Conditionals," *Linguistic Philosophy* 29 (2006): 632.
17. Ippolito, "Semantic Composition and Presupposition Projection in Subjunctive Conditionals," 634.
18. See Keith DeRose, "Can It Be That It Would Have Been Even Though It Might Not Have Been?" *Philosophical Perspectives* 13 (1999): 385–413.

NOTES 169

19. Ippolito, "Semantic Composition and Presupposition Projection in Subjunctive Conditionals," 632–634.

Chapter 6

1. An ancillary question arises from the intrinsic/extrinsic property of Lady Bracknell *having-a-nose*, as nothing pertaining to Lady Bracknell's nose—or, *indirectly*, her sense of smell—appears in the dramatic text of Wilde's 1895 play, *The Importance of Being Earnest*. Given that the character Jack says to Lady Bracknell, "you will be pleased to hear" (Wilde 1895: 298)—using the infinitive, "to hear," referring to Lady Bracknell's sense of hearing—is *having-two-ears* an intrinsic or an extrinsic property?
2. There are, of course, nonintentionalist abstractionist accounts of such creation (cf. Zvolenszky 2016; Voltolini 2020).
3. Though while less famous than Godot, there are some other important offstage characters that can reinforce the theses in this chapter: Beckett has two more famous examples of offstage characters that are quite central to the play in his *Act Without Words I* and *Act Without Words II*. Jean Genet's *The Blacks: A Clown Show*, too, with the offstage "traitor" is another important offstage character to consider as related to indeterminate identity.

Chapter 7

1. Contra Everett (2005), Woodward (2017) concludes that while it may be indeterminate to assess whether Bahrooh and Bahraah are identical, this is a matter of indeterminate *reference*, not a question of indeterminate identity. Friedell (2019) admires Woodward's line of thought, but wishes that Woodward explained the ontology of fictional characters. Friedell (2019) concludes that while Platonism may avoid positing indeterminate identity, abstract creationism—and certainly the version put forth by Evnine (2016)—is committed to indeterminate identity.
2. See Castañeda (1989).
3. There are, of course, nonintentionalist abstractionist accounts of such creation (cf. Zvolenszky 2016; Voltolini 2020).

170 NOTES

4. See, most particularly, Olf (1981) and States (1983), as well.
5. Tzachi Zamir, *Just Literature: Philosophical Criticism and Justice* (London: Routledge, 2019), 12.
6. Jerrold Levinson, *Music in the Moment* (Ithaca, NY: Cornell University Press, 1997).
7. Noël Carroll, "Performance," *Formations* 3, no. 1 (1986): 63–81.
8. Noël Carroll, *The Philosophy of Motion Pictures* (Hoboken, NJ: Wiley-Blackwell, 2008).
9. Hamilton, "The Role of Inductive Reasoning in the Evolution of Conventions," *Law and Philosophy* 17 (1998): 380–388, at 95. Hamilton plays off Robert Sugden's model for analyzing discovery situations.
10. Hamilton "The Role of Inductive Reasoning in the Evolution of Conventions," 97.
11. Hamilton "The Role of Inductive Reasoning in the Evolution of Conventions," 97.
12. Hamilton "The Role of Inductive Reasoning in the Evolution of Conventions," 98.
13. Hamilton "The Role of Inductive Reasoning in the Evolution of Conventions," 100.
14. Bennett (2017): 105–106.
15. This example is similar to Angelika Kratzer's notions of "lumps" of thought. For more on how thoughts are "lumped" together for conceptual coherence, see Kratzer (1989), as well as Kratzer (2002), for Kratzer's own modifications to her earlier theory about "lumping."

Conclusion

1. Büchner (1835): 28.
2. Büchner (1835): 28.
3. Lowercase a, b, and c are for arbitrary particulars; uppercase F, G, and H are for arbitrary properties/R for relations; p, q, and r are for propositions; x, y, and z are for individual variables; S, T, and U are for individuals/persons.
4. As noted by Inan, there is scant discussion of curiosity in philosophy (2012: xii–xiii). William James proposes an inchoate earlier version of the claims of Inan (2012), as James claims curiosity is the drive for "better cognition" (James 1899, qtd. in Kidd and Hayden 2015: 449). Celeste Kidd

and Benjamin Y. Hayden interpret "better cognition" to mean the understanding of what one does not know (2015: 449). In addition to offering the above-noted ways to view how epistemology and philosophy of language intersect to offer insights into curiosity about the knowledge that one does not possess, Inan also demonstrates how philosophy has informed both commonplace understandings and dictionary definitions of curiosity (2012: 2–6). In reviewing recent work on curiosity by historians of science and cultural critics, including Inan (2012), Richard Phillips claims that two strands of thought have been exposed on curiosity: "care" and "questions" (2015: 149).

Outside of philosophy's very limited treatment of curiosity, the fields of psychology and neuroscience also have, and more so recently, theorized the phenomenon of curiosity in humans (though the study of curiosity in animals has a richer history). Kidd and Hayden (2015) offer a summary of theories of curiosity, dividing contemporary views of curiosity into two main lines of inquiry by psychologists and neuroscientists. Lowenstein (1994) and Oudeyer and Kaplan (2007) claim, as categorized and interpreted by Kidd and Hayden, that curiosity is "an intrinsic drive," and, "is a special form of information-seeking distinguished by the fact that it is internally motivated" (Kidd and Hayden 2015: 450). Noting the problems of determining whether an action is motivated by *intrinsic* or *extrinsic* factors, Kidd and Hayden favor the more general idea of curiosity as *information-seeking*, and that describing the current state of work on curiosity research should be examined through a simplified version of the four scientific questions posed by Tingergen (1963) that help explain particular behaviors: function, evolution, mechanism, and development (Kidd and Hayden 2015: 450). Kidd and Hayden conclude that too much work has focused on taxonomy and delineating what is, or is not, curiosity (2015: 456).

Bibliography

Arciniegas, David B. "Psychosis." 21, no. 3 (2015):715–736.

Ackerman, Alan, and Martin Puchner, eds. *Against Theatre: Creative Destructions on the Modernist Stage.* New York: Palgrave Macmillan, 2006.

Alward, Peter. "Description, Disagreement, and Fictional Names." *Canadian Journal of Philosophy* 41, no. 3 (September 2011): 423–448.

Amoretti, M. Cristina, and Gerhard Preyer. "Introduction: Mind, Knowledge, and Communication in Triangular Externalism." In *Triangulation: From an Epistemological Point of View,* edited by M. Cristina Amoretti and Gerhard Preyer. Boulder, CO: Ontos, 2011.

Aristotle. *Poetics* (c. 330s BCE). Translated by Anthony Kenny. Oxford: Oxford University Press, 2013.

Armstrong, D. M. *A Combinatorial Theory of Possibility.* Cambridge: Cambridge University Press, 1989.

Arregui, Ana. "On Similarity on Counterfactuals." *Linguistics and Philosophy* 32 (2009): 245–278.

Aston, Elaine, and George Savona. *Theatre as Sign System: A Semiotics of Text and Performance* London: Routledge, 1991.

Auerbach, Erich. *Mimesis: The Representation of Reality in Western Literature.* Translated by Willard R. Trask. Princeton, NJ: Princeton University Press, (1946) 2014.

Auslander, Philip. *Liveness: Performance in a Mediatized Culture.* London: Routledge, 1999.

Austin, J. L. *How to Do Things with Words: The William James Lectures.* Edited by J. O. Urmson. Oxford: Oxford University Press, 1962.

Bach, K. "Speech Acts." In *Routledge Encyclopedia of Philosophy.* London: Routledge, 2003.

Bacon, Francis. *Novum Organum.* Edited and translated by Basil Montague. In *The Works,* 3 vols. Philadelphia: Parry & MacMillan, 1854.

Badiou, Alain. "Rhapsody for the Theatre: A Short Philosophical Treatise." *Theatre Survey* 49, no. 2 (2008): 187–238.

Beckett, Samuel. *Waiting for Godot.* New York: Grove Press, 1954.

Bennett, Michael Y. *Analytic Philosophy and the World of the Play.* London: Routledge, 2017.

Bennett, Michael Y. "In Defense of Abstract Creationism: A Recombinatorial Approach." *Philosophy and Literature* 45, no. 2 (October 2021): 489–495.

174 BIBLIOGRAPHY

Bennett, Michael Y. "Intrinsic-Extrinsic Properties in Theatre." *Philosophy and Literature* 45, no. 1 (April 2021): 34–38.

Bennett, Michael Y. *Narrating the Past through Theatre: Four Crucial Texts.* New York: Palgrave Macmillan, 2012.

Bennett, Michael Y. *The Problems of Viewing Performance.* 2021.

Bennett, Michael Y. "Propositions in Theatre: Theatrical Utterances as Events." *Journal of Literary Semantics* 47, no. 2 (November 2018): 147–152.

Bennett, Michael Y. *Reassessing the Theatre of the Absurd: Camus, Beckett, Ionesco, Genet, and Pinter.* New York: Palgrave Macmillan, 2011.

Bennett, Michael Y. *Words, Space, and the Audience: The Theatrical Tension between Empiricism and Rationalism.* New York: Palgrave Macmillan, 2012.

Bennett, Susan. *Theater Audiences: A Theory of Production and Reception.* London: Routledge, 1990.

Berto, Francesco. "Modal Meinongianism and Fiction: The Best of Three Worlds." *Philosophical Studies* 152 (2011): 316–321.

Bixby, Patrick. *Nietzsche and Irish Modernism.* Manchester: Manchester University Press, 2022.

Blau, Herbert. *The Audience.* Baltimore: Johns Hopkins University Press, 1990.

Brand, M. "Particulars, Events, and Actions." In *Action Theory: Proceedings of the Winnipeg Conference on Human Action*, edited by M. Brand and D. Walton, 133–158. Dordrecht: Reidel, 1976.

Braun, David. "Empty Names, Fictional Names, Mythical Names." *Nous* 39, no. 4 (2005): 596–631.

Bricker, Phillip. "Reducing Possible Worlds to Language." *Philosophical Studies* 52 (1987): 331–355.

Brock, Stuart. "The Creationist Fiction: The Case against Creationism about Fictional Characters." *Philosophical Review* 119 (2010): 337–364.

Brock, Stuart. "Fictionalism about Fictional Characters." *Nous* 36, no. 1 (2002): 1–21.

Brock, Stuart. "A Recalcitrant Problem for Abstract Creationism." *The Journal of Aesthetics and Art Criticism* 76 (2018): 93–98.

Brook, Peter. *The Empty Space.* New York: Atheneum, 1968.

Bryne, A. "The Epistemic Significance of Experience." *Philosophical Studies* 173, no. 4 (2016): 947–967.

Butler, Judith. "Performative Acts and Gender Constitution: An Essay in Phenomenology and Feminist Theory." *Theatre Journal* 40, no. 4 (1988): 519–531.

Camp, Pannill. *The First Frame: Theater Space in Enlightenment France.* Cambridge: Cambridge University Press, 2014.

Camp, Pannill. "The Trouble with Phenomenology." *Journal of Dramatic Theory and Criticism* 19, no. 1 (2014): 79–97.

Carlson, Marvin. *The Haunted Stage: The Theater as Memory Machine.* Ann Arbor: University of Michigan Press, 2003.

BIBLIOGRAPHY   175

Carlson, Marvin. *Performance: A Critical Introduction*. 3rd ed. London: Routledge, 2018.

Carlson, Marvin. *Shattering Hamlet's Mirror: Theatre and Reality*. Ann Arbor: University of Michigan Press, 2016.

Carlson, Marvin. *Theater Semiotics: Signs of Life*. Bloomington: Indiana University Press. 1990.

Carlson, Marvin. *Theories of the Theater: A Historical and Critical Survey from the Greeks to the Present*. Ithaca, NY: Cornell University Press, 1993.

Carroll, Noël. "Interpretation, Theatrical Performance, and Ontology." *The Journal of Aesthetics and Art Criticism* 59, no. 3 (2001): 313–316.

Carroll, Noël. "Performance." *Formations* 3, no. 1 (1986): 63–81.

Carroll, Noël. *The Philosophy of Motion Pictures*. Hoboken, NJ: Wiley-Blackwell, 2008.

Castañeda, Hector-Neri. *Thinking, Language, and Experience*. Minneapolis: University of Minnesota Press, 1989.

Chisholm, Roderick M. "Identity through Possible Worlds: Some Questions." In *The Possible and the Actual: Readings in the Metaphysics of Modality*, edited by Michael J. Loux. Ithaca, NY: Cornell University Press, 1979.

Chisholm, R. M. *Theory of Knowledge*. Englewood Cliffs, NJ: Prentice Hall, 1966/1977/1989.

Cohen, Shai. "On the Semantics of *Too* and *Only*: Distinctness and Subsumption." PhD dissertation, University of Massachusetts, Amherst, 2009.

Coleridge, Samuel Taylor. *Biographia Literaria: The Collected Works of Samuel Taylor Coleridge, Biographical Sketches of My Literary Life & Opinions*. Edited by James Engell and W. Jackson Bate. Princeton, NJ: Princeton University Press, (1817) 1983.

"Creation." *Oxford English Dictionary*. Oxford: Oxford University Press.

Cresswell, M. J. *Logics and Languages*. London: Methuen, 1973.

Cull, Laura. "Performance as Philosophy: Responding to the Problem of 'Application.'" *Theater Research International* 37, no. 1 (2012): 20–27.

Cull Ó Maoilearca, Laura. "Notes toward the Philosophy of Theatre." *Anglia* 136, no. 1 (2018): 11–42.

Culler, Jonathan. "Fabula and Sjuzhet in the Analysis of Narrative." *Poetics Today* 1, no. 3 (Spring 1980): 27–37.

Currie, Gregory. *The Nature of Fiction*. Cambridge: Cambridge University Press, 1990.

Curtis, Neal. "The Human, *In Medio*." *Angelaki* 15, no. 2 (2010): 69–84.

Davidson, Donald. *Subjective, Intersubjective, Objective*. Oxford: Oxford University Press, 2001.

Davidson, Donald. "What Metaphors Mean." *Critical Inquiry* 5, no. 1 (1978): 31–47.

Davies, David. "Fictional Truth and Fictional Authors." *British Journal of Aesthetics* 36, no. 1 (1996): 43–55.

176 BIBLIOGRAPHY

Davis, Tracy C., and Thomas Postlewait, eds. *Theatricality*. Cambridge: Cambridge University Press, 2004.

de Beistegui, Miguel. *Aesthetics After Metaphysics: From Mimesis to Metaphor*. London: Routledge, 2012.

de Marinis, Marco. *The Semiotics of Performance*. Translated by Aine O'Healy. Bloomington: Indiana University Press, 1993.

Degani-Raz, Irit. "Possible Worlds and the Concept of 'Reference' in the Semiotics of Theater." *Semiotica* 147, no. 1/4 (2003): 307–329.

Degani-Raz, Irit. "Theatrical Fictional Worlds, Counterfactuals, and Scientific Thought Experiments." *Semiotica* 157, no. 1/4 (2005): 353–375.

DeRose, Keith. "Can It Be That It Would Have Been Even Though It Might Not Have Been?" *Philosophical Perspectives* 13 (1999): 385–413.

Diamond, Elin. *Unmaking Mimesis: Essays on Feminism and Theatre*. New York: Routledge, 1997.

Diamond, Elin. *Writing Performances*. London: Routledge, 1995.

Diderot, Denis. *Diderot: Selected Writings on Art and Literature*. New York: Penguin Books, 1994.

Dilworth, John. "The Fictionality of Plays." *The Journal of Aesthetics and Art Criticism* 60, no. 3 (Summer 2002): 263–273.

Dilworth, John. "Theater, Representation, Types, and Interpretation." *American Philosophical Quarterly* 39, no. 2 (April 2002): 197–209.

Dodd. C. H. *Parables*. 1965.

Dolan, Jill. *Utopia in Performance: Finding Hope at the Theater*. Ann Arbor: University of Michigan Press, 2005.

Donnellan, Keith. "Reference and Definite Descriptions." *The Philosophical Review* 75, no. 3 (July 1966): 281–304.

Dorhn, Daniel. "Counterfactual Narrative Explanation." *The Journal of Aesthetics and Art Criticism* 67, no. 1 (Winter 2009).

Einheuser, Iris. "Some Remarks on 'Language-Created Entities.'" *Acta Analytica* 24 (2008): 185–192.

Elam, Keir. *The Semiotics of Theater and Drama*. London: Routledge, 1980.

Erickson, J. "On Mimesis (and Truth) in Performance." *Journal of Dramatic Theory and Criticism* 23 (2009): 21–38.

Everett, A. "Against Fictional Realism." *Journal of Philosophy* 102 (2005): 624–649.

Everett, Anthony. "Pretense, Existence, and Fictional Objects." *Philosophy and Phenomenological Research* 74, no. 1 (January 2007): 56–80.

Evnine, Simon. *Making Objects and Events: A Hylomorphic Theory of Artifacts, Actions, and Organisms*. Oxford: Oxford University Press, 2016.

Feit, Neil. "Naming and Nonexistence." *The Southern Journal of Philosophy* 47 (2009): 239–262.

Feldman, R. "An Alleged Defect in Gettier Counterexamples." *Australasian Journal of Philosophy* 52 (1974): 68–69.

BIBLIOGRAPHY 177

Fischer-Lichte, Erika. *The Semiotics of Theater*. Translated by Jeremy Gaines and Doris L. Jones. Bloomington: Indiana University Press, 1992.

Fischer-Lichte, Ericka. *The Transformative Power of Performance: A New Aesthetics*. Translated by Saskya Iris Jain. London: Routledge, 2008.

Friedell, David. "Abstract Creationism and Authorial Intention." *The Journal of Aesthetics and Art Criticism* 74 (2016): 129–137.

Friedell, David. "Fiction and Indeterminate Identity." *Analysis* 80, no. 2 (April 2020): 221–229.

Friedell, David. "A Problem for All of Creation." *The Journal of Aesthetics and Art Criticism* 76 (2018): 98–101.

Friedell, David. "Why Can't I Change Bruckner's *Eighth Symphony?*" *Philosophical Studies* 177 (2020): 805–882.

Friend, S. "The Real Foundation of Fictional Worlds." *Australasian Journal of Philosophy* 95, no. 1 (2017): 29–42.

Gadamer, Hans-Greorg. *Truth and Method*. Translated by Joel Weinsheimer and Donald G. Marshall. New York: Continuum, 1960.

Garner, Jr., Stanton B. *Bodied Spaces: Phenomenology and Performance in Contemporary Drama*. Ithaca, NY: Cornell University Press, 1994.

Geach, P. T. *Reference and Generality*. 3rd ed. Ithaca, NY: Cornell University Press, 1980.

Gendler, T. S. "The Puzzle of Imaginative Resistance." *Journal of Philosophy* 95, no. 1 (2000): 55–81.

Gettier, Edmund L. "Is Justified True Belief Knowledge?" *Analysis* 23, no. 6 (June 1963): 121–123.

Gibson, John. "Interpreting Words, Interpreting Worlds." *The Journal of Aesthetics and Art Criticism* 64, no. 4 (Fall 2006): 439–450.

Gluer, K. "In Defence of a Doxastic Account of Experience." *Mind and Language* 24 (2009): 297–373.

Gobert, Darren R. *The Mind-Body Stage: Passion and Interaction in the Cartesian Theater*. Stanford, CA: Stanford University Press, 2013.

Goffman, Erving. *The Presentation of Self in Everyday Life*. New York: Doubleday, 1959.

Goldman, Alvin. "Discrimination and Perceptual Knowledge." *Journal of Philosophy* 73 (1976): 771–791.

Goldman, Michael. "'Hamlet': Entering the Text." *Theatre Journal* 44, no. 4 (December 1992): 449–460.

Golub, Spencer. *Incapacity: Wittgenstein, Anxiety, and Performance Behavior*. Evanston, IL: Northwestern University Press, 2014.

Goodman, Nelson. *Languages of Art: An Approach to a Theory of Symbols*. Indianapolis: Bobbs-Merrill, 1968.

Goodman, Nelson. *Ways of Worldmaking*. Indianapolis: Hackett, 1978.

Grafton-Cardwell, Patrick. "How to Understand the Completion of Art." *The Journal of Aesthetics and Art Criticism* 78 (2020): 197–208.

178   BIBLIOGRAPHY

Guo, Yuchen. "What Is Acting?" *Journal of Aesthetics and Art Criticism* 80, no. 1 (Winter 2022): 58–69.

Hájek, Alan, and Stephan Hartmann. "Bayesian Epistemology." In *A Companion to Epistemology*, edited by J. Dancy et al., 94–106. Oxford: Blackwell, 2010.

Hamilton, James R. *The Art of Theater*. Malden, MA: Blackwell, 2007.

Hamilton, James R. "From the Author's Perspective: The Art of Theater." American Society for Aesthetics. https://aesthetics-online.site-ym.com/page/HamiltonTheater.

Hamilton, James R. "The Philosophy of Theater." *Stanford Encyclopedia of Philosophy*. 2019. https://plato.stanford.edu/entries/theater/.

Hamilton, James R. "The Text-Performance Relation in Theater." *Philosophy Compass* (2009).

Hamilton, James R. "Theatrical Performance and Interpretation." *The Journal of Aesthetics and Art Criticism* 59, no. 3 (2001): 307–312.

Hartmann, Stephan, and Jan Sprenger. "Bayesian Epistemology." In *Routledge Companion to Epistemology*. London: Routledge, 2010.

Hegel, George Wilhelm Friedrich. *Introductory Lectures on Aesthetics*. Translated by Bernard Bosanquet. New York: Penguin Books, 1993.

Hetherington, S. *Good Knowledge, Bad Knowledge: On Two Dogmas of Epistemology*. Oxford: Oxford University Press, 2001.

Hetherington, S. *Knowledge Puzzles: An Introduction to Epistemology*. Boulder, CO: Westview Press, 1996.Hills, David. "Metaphor." *Stanford Encyclopedia of Philosophy*. 2017. https://plato.stanford.edu/entries/metaphor.

Horace. *Ars Poetica* (c. 15 BCE). http://www.gutenberg.org/ebooks/9175.

Horwich, Paul. *Meaning*. Oxford: Oxford University Press, 1998.

Iacona, Andrea. "Validity and Interpretation." *Australasian Journal of Philosophy* 88, no. 2 (June 2010): 247–264.

"Imagination." *Oxford English Dictionary*. Oxford: Oxford University Press.

Inan, Ilhan. *The Philosophy of Curiosity*. New York: Routledge, 2012.

Ippolito, Michela. "Semantic Composition and Presupposition Projection in Subjunctive Conditionals." *Linguistic Philosophy* 29 (2006): 631–672.

Isherwood, Charles. "A Stylish Monster Conquers at a Glance: 'The Importance of Being Earnest." *The New York Times* (Jan. 13, 2011).

Jacquette, D. *Meinongian Logic: The Semantics of Existence and Nonexistence*. Berlin: De Gruyter, 1996.

Kania, Andrew. "Worlds Are Colliding?: Explaining the Fictional in Terms of the Real." *Philosophical Studies* 135 (2007): 65–71.

Keefe, R., and Smith, P., eds. *Vagueness: A Reader*. Cambridge, MA: The MIT Press, 1996.

Kelleher, Joe. *The Illuminated Theatre: Studies on the Suffering of Images*. Abington: Routledge, 2015.

Kennedy, Dennis. *The Spectator and the Spectacle*. Cambridge: Cambridge University Press, 2009.

BIBLIOGRAPHY 179

Kidd, Celeste, and Benjamin Y. Hayden. "The Psychology and Neuroscience of Curiosity." *Neuron* 88 (2015): 449–460.

Kolodny, Niko, and John MacFarlane. "Ifs and Oughts." *The Journal of Philosophy* 107, no. 3 (March 2010): 115–143.

Kornhaber, David. *The Birth of Theater from the Spirit of Philosophy: Nietzsche and the Modern Drama*. Evanston, IL: Northwestern University Press, 2016.

Kornhaber, David. *Theatre & Knowledge*. New York: Red Globe Press, 2020.

Krasner, David. "Empathy and Theater." In *Staging Philosophy: Intersections of Theater, Performance, and Philosophy*, 255–277. Ann Arbor: University of Michigan Press, 2006.

Krasner, David, and David Saltz, eds. *Staging Philosophy: Intersections of Theater, Performance and Philosophy*. Michigan: University of Michigan Press, 2006.

Kratzer, Angelika. "Facts: Particulars or Information Units?" *Linguistics and Philosophy* 25 (2002): 655–670.

Kratzer, Angelika. "An Investigation of the Lumps of Thought." *Linguistics and Philosophy* 12 (1989): 607–653.

Kratzer, Angelika. "Situations in Natural Language Semantics." *Stanford Encyclopedia of Philosophy* (2019). https://plato.stanford.edu/entries/situations-semantics/.

Kripke, Saul. *Naming and Necessity*. Cambridge, MA: Harvard University Press, 1980.

Kripke, Saul. "Vacuous Names and Fictional Entities." In *Philosophical Troubles Collected Papers*, Vol. 1, 52–74. New York: Oxford University Press, 2011.

Kyle, Christopher D. "Epistemicism and the Problem of Arbitrariness for Vagueness." *Dialogue* (October 2012): 54–64.

Landes, Jürgen. "Bayesian Epistemology." *Oxford Bibliographies* (2021). https://www.oxfordbibliographies.com/display/document/obo-978019 5396577/obo-9780195396577-0417.xml.

Lehrer, Keith. "Knowledge, Truth and Evidence." *Analysis* 25 (1965): 168–175.

Lehrer, Keith. "Why Not Scepticism?" *The Philosophical Forum* 2 (1971): 283–298.

Levinson, Jerrold. *Music in the Moment*. Ithaca, NY: Cornell University Press, 1997.

Levy, A. 1956. "Theatre Arts, August." *Casebook on Waiting for Godot*. Edited by Ruby Cohn, 74–78. New York: Grove Press, 1967.

Lewis, David K. *Counterfactuals*. Cambridge, MA: Harvard University Press, 1976.

Lewis, David. "Counterpart Theory and Quantified Modal Logic." In *The Possible and the Actual: Readings in the Metaphysics of Modality*, edited by Michael J. Loux. Ithaca, NY: Cornell University Press, 1979.

Lewis, David. "Elusive Knowledge." *Australasian Journal of Philosophy* 74 (1996): 549–567.

Lewis, David. *On the Plurality of Worlds*. Oxford: Basil Blackwell, 1987.

180 BIBLIOGRAPHY

Liggins, David. "Modal Fictionalism and Possible-Worlds Discourse." *Philosophical Studies* 138 (2008): 151–160.

"Live." *Merriam-Webster's Dictionary*.

Lormand, Eric. "*Qualia!* (Now Showing at a Theater Near You)." *Philosophical Topics* 22 (1994): 127–156.

Lycan, W. G. "Evidence One Does Not Possess." *Australasian Journal of Philosophy* 55 (1977): 114–126.

Lycan, W. G. "On the Gettier Problem Problem." In *Epistemology Futures*. edited by S. Hetherington. Oxford: Oxford University Press, 2006.

Lycan, William. "The Trouble with Possible Worlds." In *The Possible and the Actual: Readings in the Metaphysics of Modality*, edited by Michael J. Loux, 274–316. Ithaca, NY: Cornell University Press, 1979.

Mackie, Penelope, and Mark Jago. "Transworld Identity." In *The Stanford Encyclopedia of Philosophy* (Fall 2013 edition), edited by Edward N. Zalta. http://plato.stanford.edu/archives/fall2013/entries/identity-transworld/.

Martí, Genoveva. "The Question of Rigidity in New Theories of Reference." *Noûs* 37, no. 1 (2003): 161–179.

McAuley, Gay. *Space in Performance: Making Meaning in the Theater*. Ann Arbor: University of Michigan Press, 2000.

McFague, Sallie. *Speaking in Parables: A Study in Metaphor and Theology*. Philadelphia: Fortress Press, 1975.

McGonigal, Andrew. "Metaphor, Indeterminacy, and Intention." *British Journal of Aesthetics* 42, no. 2 (April 2002): 179–190.

Meinong, A. "The Theory of Objects." Translated by Isaac Levi, D. B. Terrell, and Roderick Chisholm. In *Realism and the Background of Phenomenology*, edited by Roderick Chisholm, 76–117. Atascadero, CA: Ridgeview, 1981.

Meinong, A. "Über Gegenstandstheorie." In *Untersuchung zur Gegenstandstheorie und Psychologie*, edited by A. Meinong, 1–51. Leipzig: J. A. Barth, 1904.

"Mirror." *Oxford English Dictionary*. 2nd ed. Oxford: Oxford University Press, 1989.

Mole, Christopher. "Fiction's Ontological Commitments." *The Philosophical Forum* (2009): 473–488.

Moser, P. K., ed. *Empirical Knowledge: Readings in Contemporary Epistemology*. Totowa, NJ: Rowman & Littlefield, 1986.

Nietzsche, Friedrich. *The Birth of Tragedy: Out of the Spirit of Music*. New York: Penguin Books, (1872) 1994.

Olf, Julian M. "Acting and Being: Some Thoughts about Metaphysics and Modern Performance Theory." *Theatre Journal* 33, no. 1 (1981): 34–45.

Olf, Julian. "Reading the Dramatic Text for Production." *Theatre Topics* 7, no. 2 (1997): 153–169.

Orlando, Eleonora. "Fictional Names without Fictional Objects." *Crítica* 40, no. 120 (December 2008): 111–127.

BIBLIOGRAPHY 181

Osipovich, David. "What Is Theatrical Performance?" *Journal of Aesthetics and Art Criticism* 64, no. 4 (2006): 461–470.

Pappas, G. S., and M. Swain, eds. *Essays on Knowledge and Justification*. Ithaca, NY: Cornell University Press, 1978.

Phillips, Richard. "Curiosity: Care, Virtue and Pleasure in Uncovering the New." *Theory, Culture & Society* 32 (2015): 149–161.

Pinillos, N. A. "Counting and Indeterminate Identity." *Mind* 112 (2003): 35–50.

Quine, W. V. "Ontological Relativity." *The Journal of Philosophy* 65, no. 7 (April 1968): 185–212.

Quine, W. V. O. "Propositional Objects." *Ontological Relativity and Other Essays*, 139–160. New York: Columbia University Press, 1968.

Parks, Suzan-Lori. *Topdog/Underdog* . New York: Theatre Communications Group, 2001.

Parsons, T. *Nonexistent Objects*. New Haven, CT: Yale University Press, 1980.

Pavel, Thomas. *Fictional Worlds*. Cambridge, MA: Harvard University Press, 1985.

Pavis, Patrice. *Languages of the Stage: Essays in the Semiology of the Theatre*. New York: Performing Arts Journal Publications, 1982.

Phelan, Peggy. *Unmarked: The Politics of Performance*. London: Routledge, 1993.

Pianesi, Fabio, and Achille C. Varzi. *Speaking of Events*. Edited by Fabio Pianesi et al. Oxford: Oxford University Press, 2000.

Plato. *The Republic* (c. 375 BCE). 2nd ed. New York: Penguin Books, 2007.

"Present." *Oxford English Dictionary*. 2nd ed. Oxford: Oxford University Press, 1989.

Priest, G. *Towards Non-Being: The Logic and Metaphysics of Intentionality*. Oxford: Oxford University Press, 2005.

Proudfoot, Diane. "Possible Worlds Semantics and Fiction." *Journal of Philosophical Logic* 35 (2006): 9–40.

Puchner, Martin. "Afterword: Please Mind the Gap between Theatre and Philosophy." *Modern Drama* 56, no. 4 (2013): 540–553.

Puchner, Martin. *The Drama of Ideas: Platonic Provocations in Theater and Philosophy*. Oxford: Oxford University Press, 2010.

Rayner, Alice. *To Act, To Do, To Perform: Drama and the Phenomenology of Action*. Ann Arbor: University of Michigan Press, 1994.

"Re-." *Oxford English Dictionary*. 2nd ed. Oxford: Oxford University Press, 1989.

Rini, A. A., and M. J. Cresswell. *The World-Time Parallel*. Cambridge: Cambridge University Press, 2012.

Rokem, Freddie. *Philosophers and Thespians: Thinking Performance*. Stanford, CA: Stanford University Press, 2010.

Rosen, Gideon. "Modal Fictionalism." *Mind* 99, no. 395 (July 1990): 327–354.

Roth, M. D., and Galis, L., eds. *Knowing: Essays in the Analysis of Knowledge*. New York: Random House, 1970.

182 BIBLIOGRAPHY

Rousseau, Jean-Jacques. *The Major Political Writings of Jean-Jacques Rousseau: The Two 'Discourses' and the 'Social Contract.'"* Chicago: University of Chicago Press, 2012.

Routley, R. *Exploring Meinong's Jungle and Beyond.* Canberra: Australian National University, 1980.

Russell, Bertrand. "On Denoting." *Mind* 14, no. 56 (October 1905): 479–493.

Russell, Bertrand. *The Problems of Philosophy.* London: Oxford University Press, 1967.

Sack, Daniel. *After Live: Possibility, Potentiality, and the Future of Performance.* Ann Arbor: University of Michigan Press, 2015.

Salis, Fiora. "Fictional Reports: A Study on the Semantics of Fictional Names." *Theoria* 68 (2010): 175–185.

Saltz, David. "From Semiotics to Philosophy: Daring to ask the Obvious." *Performance Philosophy* 1 (2015): 95–105.

Saltz, David Z. "How to Do Things on Stage." *The Journal of Aesthetics and Art Criticism* 49, no. 1 (1991): 31–45.

Saltz, David Z. "The Reality of Doing: Real Speech Acts in the Theater." In *Method Acting Reconsidered: Theory, Practice, Future,* edited by David Krasner, 61–79. New York: St. Martin's, 2000.

Saltz, David Z. "What Theatrical Performance Is (Not): The Interpretation Fallacy." *The Journal of Aesthetics and Art Criticism* 59, no. 3 (2001): 299–306.

Saltz, David. "Why Performance Theory Needs Philosophy." *Journal of Dramatic Theory and Criticism* 16, no. 1 (2001): 149–154.

Sauchelli, Andrea. "Fictional Objects, Non-Existence, and the Principle of Characterization." *Philosophical Studies* 159 (2012): 139–146.

Saussure, Ferdinand de. *Course in General Linguistics.* Translated by Roy Harris. Peru, IL: Open Court, 1986.

Schechner, Richard. *Performance Theory.* 2nd ed. London: Routledge, 1988.

Scheffler, Israel. *Symbolic Worlds: Art, Science, Language, and Ritual.* Cambridge: Cambridge University Press, 1996.

Schiller, Frederich. *On the Aesthetic Education of Man.* Translated by Reginald Snell. New York: Dover, (1795) 2004.

Schnieder B., von Solodkoff T. "In Defense of Fictional Realism." *Philosophical Quarterly* 59 (2009): 138–149.

Searle, John R. "Proper Names." *Mind* 67 (1958): 166–173.

Schipper, Jeremy. *Parables and Conflict in the Hebrew Bible.* Cambridge: Cambridge University Press, 2009.

Shope, R. K. *The Analysis of Knowing: A Decade of Research.* Princeton, NJ: Princeton University Press, 1983.

Siegel, Susanna. "The Contents of Perception" (2016). In *The Stanford Encyclopedia of Philosophy,* edited by Edward N. Zalta. https://plato.stanford.edu/entries/perception-contents.

BIBLIOGRAPHY 183

Smith, Carlota S. "Tense and Temporal Interpretation." *Lingua* 117, no. 2 (February 2007): 419–436.

"Spectatorship." Special Issue. *Theatre Journal* 66, no. 3 (October 2014).

States, Bert O. "The Actor's Presence: Three Phenomenal Modes." *Theater Journal* 35 (1983): 359–375.

States, Bert O. *Great Awakenings in Little Rooms: On the Phenomenology of Theater* Berkeley: University of California Press, 1985.

Stern, Tom. *Philosophy and Theater: An Introduction*. London: Routledge, 2014.

Stern, Tom, ed. *The Philosophy of Theatre, Drama, and Acting*. London: Rowman & Littlefield International, 2017.

Stokke, Andreas. "Fiction and Importation." *Linguistics and Philosophy* 45, no. 1 (2021): 65–89.

Stone, Jim. "Harry Potter and the Spectre of Imprecision." *Analysis* 70, no. 4 (October 2010): 638–644.

Strawson, P. F. "On Referring." *Mind* 59, no. 235 (July 1950): 320–344.

Sullivan, A. "Rigid Designation, Direct Reference, and Modal Metaphysics." *Pacific Philosophical Quarterly* 86 (2005): 577–599.

"Symposium: 'Categories of Art' at 50." *Journal of Aesthetics and Art Criticism* 78, no. 1 (Winter 2020): 65–84.

Talbott, William. "Bayesian Epistemology." In *The Stanford Encyclopedia of Philosophy* (Winter 2016 edition), edited by Edward N. Zalta. https://plato.stanford.edu/archives/win2016/entries/epistemology-bayesian/.

Tarski, Alfred. *Introduction to Logic and to the Method of Deductive Sciences*. 2nd ed. New York: Oxford University Press, 1946.

Textor, Mark. "Sense-Only-Signs: Frege on Fictional Proper Names." *Grazer Philosophische Studien* 82 (2011): 375–400.

Thomasson, Amie L. *Fiction and Metaphysics*. Cambridge: Cambridge University Press, 1999.

Titelbaum, Michael G. *Fundamentals of Bayesian Epistemology*. Vols. I & II. Oxford: Oxford University Press, 2022.

Turner, Victor. *From Ritual to Theatre: The Human Seriousness of Play*. New York: Performing Arts Journal, 1982.

Valency, Maurice. *The Flower and the Castle: An Introduction to Modern Drama*. New York: Grosset & Dunlap, 1966.

Veltman, Frank. "Making Counterfactual Assumptions." *Journal of Semantics* 22 (2005): 159–180.

"View." *Oxford English Dictionary*. 3rd ed. Oxford: Oxford University Press, 2016.

Voltolini, Alberto. "How Fictional Works are Related to Fictional Entities." *Dialectica* 57, no. 2 (2003): 225–238.

Voltolini, Alberto. The Mark of the Mental. *Phenomenology and Mind* 4 (2020): 124–136.

184 BIBLIOGRAPHY

Walton, Kendall. "Categories of Art." *The Philosophical Review* 79, no. 3 (1970): 334–367.

Walton, Kendall. *Mimesis as Make-Believe*. Cambridge, MA: Harvard University Press, 1990.

Wilde, Oscar. *The Importance of Being Earnest and Other Plays*. Edited by Peter Raby. Oxford: Oxford University Press, 2008.

Williamson, Timothy. *Knowledge and Its Limits*. Oxford: Oxford University Press, 2000.

Wilshire, Bruce. *Role Playing and Identity: The Limits of Theatre as Metaphor*. Bloomington: Indiana University Press, 1982.Wilson, D. "Relevance and the Interpretation of Literary Works." *UCL Working Papers in Linguistics* 23 (2011): 69–80.

Wittgenstein, Ludwig. *Philosophical Investigations*. 3rd ed. Translated by G. E. M. Anscombe. New York: Pearson, 1973.

Wollheim, Richard. *Art and Its Objects*. 2nd ed. Cambridge: Cambridge University Press, 1980.

Woodruff, Paul. *The Necessity of Theater; The Art of Watching and Being Watched*. Oxford: Oxford University Press, 2008.

Woodward, Richard. "Identity in Fiction." *Philosophy and Phenomenological Research* 94 (2017): 646–671.

Woodward, Richard. "Is Modal Fictionalism Artificial?" *Pacific Philosophical Quarterly* 92 (2011): 535–560.

Woodward, Richard. "Truth in Fiction." *Philosophy Compass* 6, no. 3 (2011): 158–167.

Worthen, W. B. *Drama: Between Poetry and Performance*. Malden, MA: Wiley-Blackwell, 2010.

Zamir, Tzachi. *Acts: Theater, Philosophy, and the Performing Self*. Ann Arbor: University of Michigan Press, 2014.

Zamir, Tzachi. *Just Literature: Philosophical Criticism and Justice*. London: Routledge, 2019.

Zarrilli, Phillip B. "Toward a Phenomenological Model of the Actor's Embodied Modes of Experience." *Theater Journal* 56, no. 4 (2004): 653–666.

Zvolenszky, Zsófia. "Fictional Character, Mythical Objects, and the Phenomenon of Inadvertent Creation." *Res Philosophica* 93 (2016): 311–333.

Index

For the benefit of digital users, indexed terms that span two pages (e.g., 52–53) may, on occasion, appear on only one of those pages.

abduction, 101–2, 167–68n.7
abstract creationism
  fictional entities as abstract objects under, 39
  indeterminate identity and, 9–10, 115–17, 122
  intentionalism and, 131
  Waiting for Godot and, 122, 131
abstract objects
  existence of, 40
  fictional characters and, 41
  realists' views of, 35–36
  re-creations and, 31–32, 36, 55, 83
  re-positioned objects and, 36, 55
  theatrical performance and, 64–65
  theatrical worlds and, 24–25
  type-token relationships and, 37, 38
  Waiting for Godot and, 10–11
acting
  cross-casting and, 53
  display behavior and, 28
  fixing of a single possible world by, 52
  Guo on, 25–27, 52, 53–54
  hiding of behavior and, 27
  ludic behavior and, 29
  mimesis and, 25–26, 53–54
  performance behavior and, 28
  re-creation and, 53–54
  repetition and, 29–30

  as simultaneous remembrance and forgetting, 103–4
  subsumption and, 81, 133
aesthetics of theatre, 16, 18
Alfred Hitchcock Presents (television show), 51
allegory, 6–7, 45, 46–47
Analytic Philosophy and the World of the Play (Bennett), 23, 24–25, 31–32, 47
ancient Greece and Rome, 15–16, 18–20, 102, 132
Animal Farm (Orwell), 46
antitheatricality, 30
Archer, William, 96–97
Aristotle, 17, 19–22
Armstrong, D. M., 6–7, 24–25, 160–61n.8
Arrabal, Fernando, 107
Ars Poetica (Horace), 19–20
Art and Imagination (Scruton), 49–50
artifactualists, 34, 35–36
The Art of Theater (Hamilton), 10–11, 30, 135, 136
Auslander, Philip, 99–100
Austin, J. L., 87–88

Bach, K., 91
Bacon, Francis, 21–22
Bah-Tale (Schnieder and von Solodkoff), 115–17

186 INDEX

Bayesian epistemology, 59
Beckett, Samuel. See *Waiting for
    Godot* (Beckett)
Bedford, Brian, 112–13, 133
Berto, Francesco, 34
The Birth of Tragedy (Nietzsche), 20
Blind Men and the Elephant parable,
    55, 57–59
Borges, Jorge Luis, 67–68
Bradley, F. H., 73–74
Brand, M., 92
Brecht, Bertolt, 22, 94–95
Brock, Stuart, 39–40
Bruckner, Anton, 110
Buchner, Georg, 141–42

card games, 141–43
Carroll, Noël, 10–11, 134–35, 136
Cervantes, Miguel, 68
Cohen, Shai, 76–78
coherence theory of truth, 73–74,
    138, 151
Coleridge, Samuel Taylor, 19–20
completion pluralism, 65
concrete objects
    audience's development of
        knowledge and, 136, 137–38
    definition of, 151
    mimesis and, 22
    theatrical performance and, 65
    theatrical worlds and, 24–25
Continental philosophy, 16, 20–21
correspondence theory of truth, 73–
    74, 138, 151
counterfactual logic, 148, 149
Craig, E. Gordon, 22
Cresswell, M. J., 102
critical theory, 20–21
cross-casting
    directors' justification for, 125–26
    distinctness and, 133
    Lady Bracknell character and, 53,
        112–13, 126–27, 132
    truthfulness and, 126–27, 134

The Crucible (Miller), 46
curiosity, 11–12, 145, 170–71
Curtis, Neal, 157–59n.5

Danes, Claire, 128–29
Danton's Death (Buchner), 141–42
Davidson, Donald, 46–47, 62
deduction, 101–2
Degani-Raz, Irit, 24, 98, 101
degrees of belief, 57–60, 145–46, 151
DeRose, Keith, 105–6
Descartes, Réne, 20, 68–69
Deveare-Smith, Anna, 50–51
Diderot, Denis, 19–20
Dilworth, John, 23–24, 50
display behavior, 28
distinctness
    counting and, 77
    cross-casting and, 133
    definition of, 76, 127–28, 152
    fictional objects and, 39, 41
    Hamlet and, 10–11, 127–30
    painting apples example and, 77
    semantics and, 8
    subsumption and, 82
    teapot example and, 77–78
    truth and, 82
Dodd, C. H., 46–47
Don Quixote (Cervantes), 68
Doyle, Arthur Conan, 35, 41
The Dumb Waiter (Pinter), 109

Eighth Symphony (Bruckner), 110
The Enlightenment, 18, 19–20
epistemology of theatre
    Bayesian epistemology and, 59
    defining questions of, 16
    phenomenology of theatre and,
        17–18
    propositional attitudes and, 70–71
    qualia and, 70–71
    semiotics and, 17–18
    triangulation and, 62–64, 70–72
Everett, Anthony, 116

INDEX 187

Evnine, Simon, 110–11, 117, 122

Feagin, Susan L., 94–95
fictional incompleteness, 74–75
fictionalists, 34–35
fictional objects
 distinctness of, 39, 41
 existence of, 39–40
 plenitude of, 40, 42
Fictional Worlds (Pavel), 24
film, 138–39
Finley, Karen, 51
Fischer-Lichte, Erika, 100–1
The Flower and the Castle (Valency), 47
Friedell, David
 abstract creationism and, 39–40,
  115, 116–17
 on *Bah-Tale,* 116
 Brock's critique of, 39–40
 on contingent social practices and
  changing artistic works, 110–12
 indeterminate identity and, 9–
  10, 115–16
 on intrinsic and extrinsic
  properties of art, 9–10, 109, 112
 on metaphysics of fictional
  objects, 33
 Platonism and, 116–17
Fusco, Coco, 51

Gadamer, Hans-Georg, 17–18, 123,
 157–59n.5
Geach, Peter Thomas, 77–78
generation, 74–76, 79
Gettier Problem, 63–64, 162–63n.1,
 165n.12
The Goat (Albee), 109
Goethe, Johann Wolfgagn von, 20
Golub, Spencer, 28–29
Goodman, Nelson, 22–23, 49–50,
 159–60n.7
Grafton-Cardwell, Patrick, 65–66
Greece. *See* ancient Greece and Rome
Guernica (Arrabal), 107

Guo, Yuchen, 25–27, 52, 53–54

Hamilton, James R.
 on acting as display behavior, 28
 on audience members'
  development of common
  knowledge, 135–36
 ingredients model and, 22–23
 mimesis and, 25
 on performance as art form, 66–67
 on relationship between text and
  performance, 31–32
 spectators' common knowledge of
  theatrical events and, 10–11, 28
Hamlet (Shakespeare)
 casting of Hamlet and,
  127, 129–30
 distinctness and, 10–11, 127–30
 Hamlet as abstract object in, 41
 Hamlet as re-created object in,
  42–43
 Hamlet's madness in, 127, 128–30
 The Murder of Gonzago play in,
  8–9, 91–92
 "Necessary-Hamlet" and, 42–43
 "Possible-Hamlet" and, 43
 subsumption and, 10–11, 80, 127–30
 Yorick's skull in, 109
Hebrew Bible, 46
Hegel, G.W.F., 19–20
Heraclitus, 55, 69–70
history plays, 107
Homeland (television show), 128–29
Horace, 19–20

Ibsen, Henrik, 47–48, 102
The Importance of Being Earnest
  (Wilde). *See also* Lady Bracknell
  (character in *The Importance of
  Being Earnest*)
 intrinsic and extrinsic properties
  of, 112–14
 truth *versus* truthfulness in, 81,
  126–27, 133–34

188 INDEX

importation, 74–76, 78–79
Inan, Ilhan, 146–47, 148, 170–71n.4
indeterminate identity
  abstract creationism and, 9–10,
    115–17, 122
  offstage characters and,
    9–10, 115–16, 123–24, 130–
    31, 132–33
  onstage world of the play and,
    122–23, 131–33
  Platonism and, 116, 121, 130–31
  split indeterminate identity and,
    118–19
  Waiting for Godot and, 9–10,
    113–14, 115–16, 118–19, 120–
    24, 130–31
indeterminate reference, 9–10, 116–
  17, 130–31
ingredients model, 22–23, 27
intended creation by pretense view,
  39–40
Ippolito, Michela, 105–6
Isherwood, Charles, 112–13

*Journal of Aesthetics and Art
  Criticism,* 20–21
justified beliefs and justified true
  beliefs, 55–58, 59, 134–35

Kennedy, Dennis, 69–70
Kripke, Saul, 17, 35–36

Lady Bracknell (character in *The
  Importance of Being Earnest)*
  cross-casting of, 53, 112–13, 126–
    27, 132
  distinct properties of, 133–34
  intrinsic *versus* extrinsic
    properties of, 113–14
  nose of, 109, 113–14, 133–34
  subsumption and, 134
  trans-world identity and, 113–14
  truthfulness and, 126–27, 133–34

Lahr, Bert, 53
Languages of Art (Goodman), 22–
  23, 49–50
The Laramie Project (Kaufman),
  50–51
Lehrer, Keith, 69
Levinson, Jerrold, 10–11, 134–
  35, 136
Lewis, David, 35–36, 76, 101, 112,
  113–14, 135
"The Library of Babel" (Borges),
  67–68
The Lines Between the Lines (Rowan),
  2
liveness
  actors' remembrance and
    forgetting as foundation of,
    103–4
  actualizing of the theatrical
    counterfactual and, 103
  antecedent conditions set forth
    at the beginning of a play and,
    105–6
  mediatized performance and,
    99–100
  mimesis and, 22
  ontology of theatre and, 16, 17
  possibility and, 99, 101–2, 104–5,
    167–68n.7
  presentness and, 100–1
  theatrical language and, 103–4
  theatrical performance and, 64
  theatrical tense and, 98
  two-past mismatched
    counterfactuals, 99
logic of acquisition, 146–47, 148–49
logic of verification, 148
Long Day's Journey into Night
  (O'Neill), 137
ludic behavior, 29

The Master Builder (Ibsen), 47–48, 49
McFague, Sallie, 46–47

INDEX   189

Meinongians, 34–35
metaphor
  allegory and, 6–7, 46
  biblical scholarship and, 46–47
  brute force accounts and, 46–47
  definition of, 45
  Ibsen and, 47–48
  parables and, 46–47
  presentation and, 6–7
  re-creation and, 6–7, 50
  theatrical language and, 89
  transparency and, 49
  truth and, 46–47
metonymy, 45
mimesis
  acting and, 25–26, 53–54
  Aristotle and, 21–22
  concrete objects and, 22
  distrust of theatre and, 21–22
  imitation and, 25
  liveness and, 22
  Plato and, 17, 21–22
  theatricality and, 30
  truth and, 31
modals, 164n.7
Moore, G. E., 73–74

The Necessity of Theater (Woodruff),
    21–22, 30
New Testament, 46–47
Nietzsche, Friedrich, 19–20

offstage characters
  indeterminate identity and,
      9–10, 115–16, 123–24, 130–
      31, 132–33
  indeterminate reference and,
      130–31
  intentions of the author
      and, 123
  Waiting for Godot and, 9–10, 115–
      16, 117–18, 121–22, 127, 130
ontology of theatre, 6–7, 16, 17

parables
  The Bible and, 46
  "Blind Men and the Elephant"
      and, 55, 57–59
  brute force accounts and, 46–47
  metaphors and, 46–47
parallax effect, 62, 63–64, 152, 153
Parks, Suzan-Lori, 1–2, 143
Pavel, Thomas, 24
Peña, Guillermo-Gomez, 51
performance behavior, 28
performance
      philosophy, 16, 20–21
performance studies, 16, 20–21
performatives, 87–88
Phelan, Peggy, 20–21, 99–100
phenomenology of theatre, 17–18
"philosophical turn" in theatre
      studies, 20–21
philosophy of theatre, 15–16, 19–20
"Pierre Menard, the Author of the
      Quixote" (Borges), 67–68
Plato
  changes in artistic creations and,
      110–11
  dialogic forms of writing and, 19
  indeterminate identity and, 116,
      121, 130–31
  mimesis and, 17, 21–22
  philosophy of theatre and, 19–20
play
  antecedent conditions set forth at
      the beginning of, 105–6
  definition of, 66
  as extended counterfactual
      condition, 96–97
Poetics (Aristotle), 19, 21–22
possibilists, 34, 35–36
possible worlds thesis, 24
poststructuralism, 20–21
presentation, 6–7, 51
The Problems of Viewing Performance
      (Bennett), 7–8

190 INDEX

propositional attitudes, 70–71, 148
propositional content, 8–9, 89, 92–93

qualia, 70–71

realists, 34–36, 160–61n.8
re-creations
abstract objects and, 31–32,
36, 55, 83
acting and, 53–54
definition of, 157–59n.5
docudrama and, 25
dramatic texts and, 31–32
existence of, 40
fictional worlds and, 38–39
metaphors and, 6–7, 50
one-person shows and, 25
presentation and, 6–7
re-created objects and, 36, 42–43,
55, 83, 153
theatrical performances and,
31–32
theatrical worlds and, 6–7, 24–25
Reference Time, 104–5
The Renaissance, 18, 19–20, 145
re-positioning, 6–7, 36, 44, 55, 83,
153, 161n.9
representation, 6–7, 50–51
Republic (Plato), 21–22
revelatory speech, 94
Richards, I. A., 45
Rini, A. A., 102
Rohrbaugh, Guy, 110–11
Romanticism, 20
Rome. *See* ancient Greece and Rome
Rousseau, Jean- Jacques, 19–
20, 21–22
Rowan, Bess, 2
Russell, Bertrand, 73–74

Sack, Daniel, 101
Saltz, David, 29, 66–67, 141
sarcasm, 89

Sartre, Jean- Paul, 129
Schiller, Friedrich, 19–20
Scruton, Roger, 49–50
Searle, John, 39, 40
semiotics, 17–18, 20–21
Seneca, 19
Shakespeare, William. See *Hamlet*
(Shakespeare)
Shepard, Matthew, 50–51
Sherlock Holmes character, 35,
41, 101–2
situation semantics, 76
Situation Time, 104–5
Smith, Carlota S., 104
Smokey Joe's Cafe (musical), 70–71
sorites paradox, 76–78
Speech Act Theory, 88
Speech Time, 104–5
spells, 1–2
Staging Philosophy collection, 20–21
States, Bert O., 17–18
Stokke, Andreas, 74–76, 78–79,
133–34
structuralism, 20–21
subsumption
acting and, 81, 133
definition of, 75–76, 127–28, 152
distinctness and, 82
Hamlet and, 10–11, 80, 127–30
interpretation and, 82
painting apples example and, 76–
77, 78–79
sand example and, 76–77, 78–
79, 127
semantics and, 4–5, 8, 76
textual assertions and, 82
theatrical characters and, 10–11,
126–27, 134
theatrical language and, 94
theatrical text and, 4–5, 8, 79
truthfulness and, 8–9, 10–11,
82–83, 125
synecdoche, 45

teatri topia, 73, 141
theatre
  curiosity and, 145
  definition of, 15, 66
  rules of engagement in, 143
theatrical characters
  casting and, 119–20, 125–26
  definitional questions regarding,
    126
  distinct properties of, 126–27, 134
  dramatic texts' limiting of the
    range of, 43
  fictional characters compared to,
    33–34
  realists' views of, 35–36
  re-creation and, 6–7, 43
  subsumed properties of, 10–11,
    126–27, 134
theatricality, 30, 167n.6
theatrical language
  absurd theatre and, 95
  baseball language
    compared to, 90
  events and, 88
  history plays and, 107
  internally coherent world of the
    play and, 88
  liveness and, 103–4
  metaphor and, 89
  movable referents and, 90
  possibility and, 99
  propositional content and,
    89, 92–93
  revelatory speech and, 94
  sarcasm and, 89
  subsumption and, 94
  theatrical tense and, 98–99, 100–
    1, 102–3
theatrical performance
  abstract objects and, 64–65
  artistic objects *versus* artistic
    experience in, 67
  Bayesian epistemology and, 59

Blind Men and the Elephant
  parable and, 55, 57–59
  completion pluralism and, 65
  concrete objects and, 65
  constants *versus* variables in, 59
  degrees of belief and, 57–60, 145–
    46, 151
  individual spectator experience
    and, 68–70
  justified beliefs and justified true
    beliefs in, 55–58, 59, 134–35
  liveness and, 64
  parallax effect and, 62, 63–64,
    152, 153
  projecting beliefs and, 57
  real bodies doing real actions in, 4,
    15–16, 22, 33–34
  re-creation of theatrical characters
    and, 43
Thomasson, Amie L., 34, 35–36
tokens. *See* type-token model
Topdog/Underdog (Parks), 1–2, 143
triangulation, 7–8, 62–64, 70–72, 82,
    152, 154
truth
  distinctness and, 82
  fictional truths and, 74–75
  metaphors and, 46–47
  mimesis and, 31
  subsumed properties of theatrical
    characters and, 10–11
Truth and Method (Gadamer), 17–18
truthfulness
  cross-casting and, 126–27, 134
  definition of, 154
  history plays and, 107
  subsumed properties and, 8–9,
    10–11, 82–83, 125
  truthful properties and, 8, 79, 81–
    82, 125, 133–34, 153
two-past mismatched
    counterfactuals, 29–30,
    99, 105–6

192 INDEX

type-token model, 23, 37, 38, 50

utopias, 73, 141

Valency, Maurice, 47–49
Voltaire, 20

Waiting for Godot (Beckett)
    abstract creationism and, 122, 131
    Beckett on, 122
    dead tree in, 109
    Godot as abstract object in, 10–11
    Godot's determinate properties in,
        121, 130–32
    Godot's offstage status in,
        9–10, 115–16, 117–18, 121–22,
        127, 130
    indeterminate identity and, 9–10,
        113–14, 115–16, 118–19, 120–
        24, 130–31
    onstage action in, 117–18

possible worlds in, 53
productions (1956 and 2009)
    of, 53
Walton, Kendall L., 50
Who's Afraid of Virginia Woolf?
    (Albee), 109
Wilde, Oscar. See *The Importance of
    Being Earnest* (Wilde)
Wilson, D., 91
Wittgenstein, Ludwig, 28–29, 68–69
Wollheim, Richard, 49–50
Woodruff, Paul, 21–22, 27–
    28, 30–31
Woodward, Richard, 9–10, 116–17
Worthen, W. B., 4

Zamir, Tzachi, 10–11, 29–30, 134–
    35, 136
Zarrilli, Phillip B., 132–33
Žižek, Slavoj, 63–64
The Zoo Story (Albee), 109